SHIATSU
JAPANESE FINGER
PRESSURE THERAPY

SHIATSU

JAPANESE FINGER PRESSURE THERAPY

Do It Yourself Acupressure

by William Schultz

BELL PUBLISHING COMPANY   NEW YORK

Copyright © MCMLXXVI by William Schultz
Library of Congress Catalog Card Number: 75-10776
All rights reserved.
This edition is published by Bell Publishing Company.,
a division of Crown Publishers, Inc.,
by arrangement with Drake Publishers, Inc.

h i j k l m n o p

"No one dies from old age alone, but rather . . . worry, tension and the will to die . . . these are the killers."

ABOUT THE AUTHOR

The author was introduced to Shiatsu by an acquaintance affiliated with the State Department in Tokyo, where Schultz was living with his family. Shiatsu was suggested as a therapy for stress and tension.

So impressed with the method, Schultz enrolled as a student at the Shiatsu Institute in 1954 and in 1966 became the fifth student to obtain a Master's Degree.

During his period of study, Schultz moved his family back to the U.S., continuing his exporting business. But Schultz also continued his study and practice of Shiatsu and often helped friends to relieve their ailments with the treatment. Word spread quickly and in 1957 Schultz opened the first Shiatsu office in the U.S. in Long Beach, California.

In 1962 Schultz moved his Shiatsu office to Desert Hot Springs, California. People from all over the world have come there for treatment.

At the present writing, there are only two authentic Shiatsu practitioners in the U.S.: one in New York State and the other, Shiatsu Thera-Spa, in California.

TABLE OF CONTENTS

SHIATSU
JAPANESE FINGER
PRESSURE THERAPY

CERTIFICATE OF MASTERS
SHIATSU
FIFTH EVER ISSUED

指圧道修士

ウイリアム・シュルツ
1925 年 2 月 27 日生

上記の者指圧道に精励其の成績顕著なるもの
があり仍て本協会称号授与規程により上記の
称号を授与する

昭和 41 年 4 月 5 日

日本指圧協会長 浪越徳治郎

SHIATSU
CERTIFICATE OF ACHIEVEMENT
WILLIAM C. SCHULTZ
IS HEREWITH AWARDED THE DEGREE OF

MASTER OF SHIATSU

IN RECOGNITION OF THE GREAT TECHNICAL
ADROITNESS THAT HE HAS ATTAINED THROUGH
LONG AND DILIGENT STUDY OF THE ART AND
THE PRACTICAL APPLICATION THERE OF. WE
EXPECT HIM TO CONTINUE HIS ENDEAVOR AND
BECOME A LEADING AUTHORITY IN THE FUTURE.

TOKYO APRIL 11th 1966

TOKUJIRO NAMIKOSHI
PRESIDENT
NIPPON SHIATSU ASSOCIATION

FOREWORD

How did I learn of Shiatsu and its method of relieving minor pains and tensions? My introduction was very traumatic! For years I had suffered chronic headaches, and the only source of relief was by osteopathic or chiropractic adjustment. The introduction occurred during my tour with the Eighth Army Special Services Section, in Tokyo.

My headaches were becoming acute and the military dispensary aspirin (APC) was having no effect. After suffering for some time and not being able to find either an osteopath or chiropractor, a friend of mine suggested I take a Shiatsu treatment. This friend, a *nisei* or Japanese-American, explained that Shiatsu is a type of pressure massage and would, most likely, relieve the pain.

Although not too impressed with the idea, I was in pain and hoped it might give me some relief. I made arrangements to go. My friend, John Sato, made the appointment for me at the Nippon Shiatsu Institute in Kanda, a Tokyo suburb. Little did I realize that this would be a turning point in my life.

Up to this point, my primary concern was to find relief for my own problem, but after my first treatment, I was so enthused that as soon as it was feasible, I made arrangements to enroll as a student. I felt a tremendous compulsion to acquire this knowledge in order to help others. That was many years ago and my enthusiasm is as great today as it was then. If I may impart even a portion of this enthusiasm and knowledge to you, perhaps this will be a turning point in your life as well.

The thing that most impressed me with my first treatment was the practitioner's understanding of muscle stress and strain. Her technique pinpointed the problem in short order. She had not been told that in the Special Services Section of the Army I played drums for army shows and performed twenty- to thirty-minute drum solos, three and four times a day. Yet, she actually showed me the movements that I made with the right arm extended and my right wrist moving up and down. The movement she made was precisely as I performed during the shows.

My symptom was "acute tension." Defined, acute tension is "a chronic physical tension, combined with an emotional pressure."

This book on Shiatsu has been written specifically for those who find themselves with the "acute tension" syndrome and would like to share my understanding and techniques of Shiatsu, so that you will receive as much help as I have, whether your pains and tensions are minor or major.

There exists a sensible horizon in the field of preventative medicine. Should my own writings and observations of Shiatsu stimulate another's intellect to prove these theories, beyond my limitations, my most subtle purpose will have been accomplished.

CHAPTER ONE
METHODOLOGY
(A BIT OF HISTORY)

I. – *Shiatsu - ancient health art.*
A. Oldest written form of physical therapy.
B. Original Chinese term *tien'an.*
  1. Yellow Emperor's Dynasty (500 years B.C.)
  2. Acupuncture and acupressure appear simultaneously.
C. Acupuncture and acupressure, both integral parts of Chinese medicine.

II. – *Shiatsu - introduction to Japan 6th Century A.D.*
A. Introduced by Buddist monks.
B. Popularity due to flexibility.
  1. Affecting minor pains.
  2. Affecting major pains and disorders.

III. – *1830 Western or Aleopathic medicine introduced in Japan.*
A. Euro-American thinking becomes dominant in Japan.
B. Revival of Shiatsu by Dr. Namikoshi.
C. Full acceptance by Japanese Ministry of Health, today.
D. Nippon Shiatsu School has 20,000 graduates.

IV – *Shiatsu - appeared throughout the world.*
A. Heinrich Himmler, German Nazi leader; chief of the Gestapo, was treated by a Hungarian. (1)
B. Well-known personalities that have used the treatment: Marilyn Monroe, Joe DiMaggio, and Lefty O'Doul

V.–Shiatsu - *originally an art form.*
A. Dr. Namikoshi establishing it as a science.
B. Results are abundant scientific truths are few.

VI.–*Chinese energy flows.*
A. Foundation of acupuncture and acupressure.
B. Laws of neurology not applicable.

VII.–*Chinese medicine.*
A. Body treated as a "whole" physical and emotional.
B. Hippocrates taught same theory.

VIII.–*"Yin" and "yang" syndrome.*
A. Strong and weak, foundation of all laws.
B. Stress and strain are result of Yin and Yang syndrome.

IX.–*Endocrine and neural systems.*
A. Each system dependent upon the other.
B. Neural strong.
C. Endocrine weak and dependent.
D. Metabolic control is neural.

X.–*Nervous system.*
A. First division central and peripheral nerves.
B. Autonomic system.
   1. Sympathetic.
   2. Parasympathetic.
C. Two subsystems are balance control.

XI.–**Tsubo** - *Neural trigger points.*
A. Basic theories of Shiatsu.
B. Advanced theories Shiatsu only taught under academic conditions.

XII.–*Research in acupuncture and Shiatsu.*
A. Korea Professor Kim Bong.
   1. Bioelectric corpuscle.
   2. Atoms of the body.
   3. Electrical force-field.
B. Ties all bodily functions together.

XIII.–**Bong Corpuscles**
A. Will support psychosomatic origin of disease.
B. Central nervous system and autonomic nervous system conflict.
C. Research established as much as 70 percent of all disease starts with tension and strain. (2)

XIV.–*Tension and disease.*
A. Bacteria and viruses are fought by the body antibodies.
B. Stress and tension impair the function of the phagocytes.

C. Emotions disturb the sympathetic and parasympathetic nervous systems.
D. Autonomic upset may deploy the phagocytes to the wrong parts of the body; or a 'much to general' distribution throughout the body.

XV. – *Japanese research supports Lactic Acid transformation with Shiatsu.*
A. Lactic acid - neural waste.
B. Shiatsu pressure changes lactic acid into glycogens (energy cells).
C. Possible prevention or reduction of infection by combining the *bong corpuscle* theory and the Shiatsu *lactic acid* transformation process.
D. Shiatsu and acupuncture may well revolutionize neurology and physical therapy.

XVI. – *Do It Yourself Shiatsu* (Acupressure)
A. This book is not for systemic disorders, but simple everyday muscle tensions.
B. Serious chronic conditions should have competent help.

(1) *Reader's Digest*
(2) *Magill University*

CHAPTER TWO
APPLICATION OF THE FINGERS and KNUCKLES

*Y*ou may not know your own strength is not just a platitude when studying acupressure. There are certain dangers in applying too much pressure, and there are areas in which the application of pressure should be avoided.

This chapter is devoted to application, noting the specific amount of pressure to apply with the fingers and knuckles. Different parts of the body require a wide range of pressures. Let us consider these pressures on a scale of pounds (a unit of weight equal to sixteen ounces or seven thousand grains; also called the avoir dupois pound), so you may practice on a bathroom scale to a maximum scale of fifteen pounds.

An important point to keep in mind as you start your finger exercise is to always place the fingers that are not in use on a firm area and preferably on one that has no key pressure points. As you practice with the scale, place a solid object nearby to rest your other fingers on. (See Figure 2-1a.)

Fig. 2-1a. Method of practicing the measurement of pounds in applying pressure.

The thumbs have unusual strength and sensitivity. It is for this reason that centuries ago, the ancients selected the thumb as the key digit.

It has been necessary for me to alter the use of the thumb in some areas for the do it yourself technique.

You will notice in Figure 2-2 that the thumb turns back and utilizes the great flat area. Remember, the secret of Shiatsu is in applying the pressure. (See Figure 2-2.)

Before you actually begin your exercises, we will discuss some of the taboos in applying the pressure.

The tendency is to gouge, and this makes me tremble because

tissue can be bruised, or in some cases where there are coral-like calcium deposits, gouging can also lacerate the tissue. Occasionally a gouging motion may be required, but *not* until a probe has been made *first.*

The second of the two most common mistakes that the majority of beginners make is to use too much of the point of the thumb. Using too much of the point of the thumb risks breaking or marking the skin with the nail.

The secret of Shiatsu is in the application of the pressure. There is little or no massaging done.

When application is made, hold firmly for ten seconds and then release suddenly.

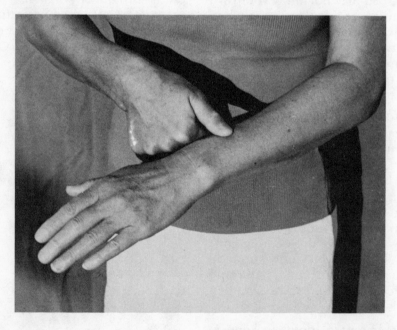

Fig. 2-1b. This photograph shows the application of the right thumb. The same process is used, in reverse, for the left thumb.

Caution: Treat any hard or in-flammed tissue with care. Should hardness or inflammation persist, seek competent help.

One of the easiest areas to first practice the thumb application is on the forearm, changing from one arm to the other.

After becoming thoroughly familiar with the method of application, the next step is to develop the pounds of pressure until you have the feel of the differing pressures.

Different people have different tolerances for pain and should a recommended pressure prove either too severe or too little, adjust accordingly. Muscular development, inherent characteristics, as well as general health, all have relative effects on a person's tolerance level. Mrs. Nakamura, one of my instructors at the Nippon Shiatsu Institute, was very adamant about pressure relative to a person's health and explained that a person who is acutely ill is so sensitive that on or two pounds of pressure is comparable to ten pounds applied to a healthy person.

I wish to reiterate that the ideal limb for practicing thumb pressure is the forearm, but there is another: the front side of the thigh.

Daily practice is necessary with a minimum amount of time of approximately two hours. This practice can be done while sitting and watching television. A diagram showing pressure points of the forearm can be seen in Figures 2-3.

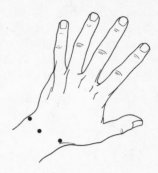

Fig. 2-2. Pressure points of the wrist.

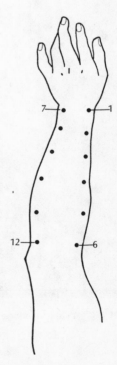

Fig. 2 - 3. Pressure points of the forearm. (Pressure: twelve pounds.)

The second most frequently used digits are the forefingers. The forefinger is more suitable for inaccessible areas, or places that do not require a great deal of pressure.

Only those with unusually strong fingers can apply more than ten pounds of pressure. The forefinger can be reinforced by the middle finger, thus increasing the pressure capability to twelve or fifteen pounds. (See Figures 2-5 and 2-6.)

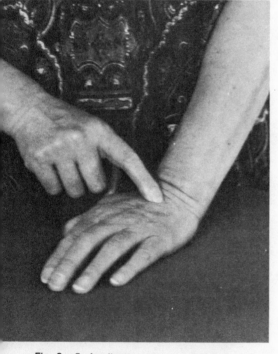

Fig. 2 - 5. Application of the forefinger.

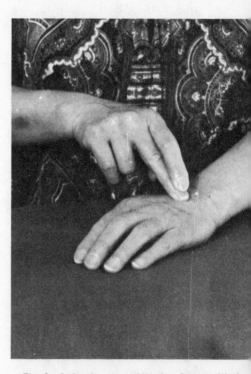

Fig. 2 - 6. Application of the forefinger with the middle finger used as reinforcement.

The middle finger alone is particularly good to use around the wrist and ankle areas. (See Figure 2-7.)

BRIEF DESCRIPTION OF THE USE OF THE MIDDLE FINGER SHOWN ALONE.

1 This covers the application of the one- and two-finger combinations. There will be other variations shown in later chapters.

Four-Finger Pressure

This technique is used primarily in the abdominal area. Usually, the fundamental use of four-finger pressure is on the opposite side of the body from the thumb pressure, thus creating a partial therapy of their own on the opposition nerve trunks. The four fingers used are, naturally, all the fingers, with out use of the thumb. (See Figure 2-8.)

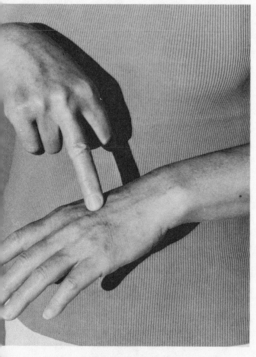

Fig. 2 7. Application of the middle finger used alone.

Fig. 2 - 8. Application of the four-finger technique in the abdominal area.

The abdominal area is a vital one, and a great deal of caution should be exercised in releasing tension here.

The four-finger technique has other uses such as the sides of the thighs and calves of the legs, as shown in Figure 2-9.

Other key areas for use of the four-finger technique are the forearm, upper arm, and shoulder. (See Figures 2-10-2-12.)

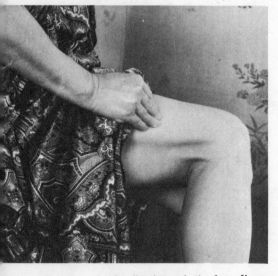

Fig. 2 - 9. Application of the four-finger technique to the legs and thigh areas.

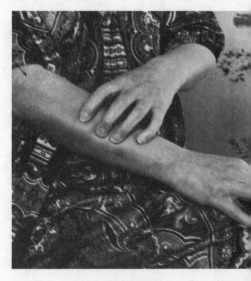

Fig. 2 - 10. Application of the four-finger techinique to the forearm area.

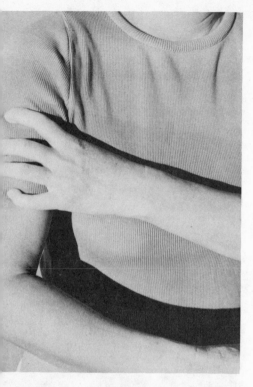

Fig. 2 - 11. Application of the four-finger technique to the upperarm area.

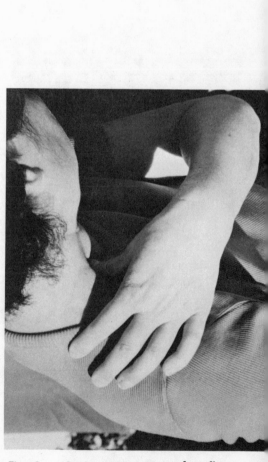

Fig. 2 - 12. Application of the four-finger technique to the shoulder area.

Knuckles may be utilized much the same way that we use the fingers. However, please keep in mind that there is no sensitivity in the knuckles. Therefore, the application must be gentle. (See Figure 2-13.)

Other areas keyed for use of the knuckles are: the outside of the thigh, the inside of the forearm, and the oblique muscles of the lower back. (See Figures 2-14-2-16.)

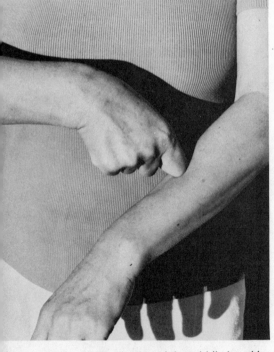

Fig. 2 - 13. Application of the middle knuckle of the forefinger to the forearm area.

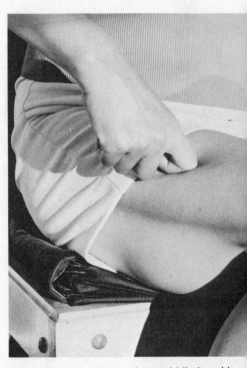

Fig. 2 - 14. Application of the middle knuckle of the forefinger to the outside of the thigh.

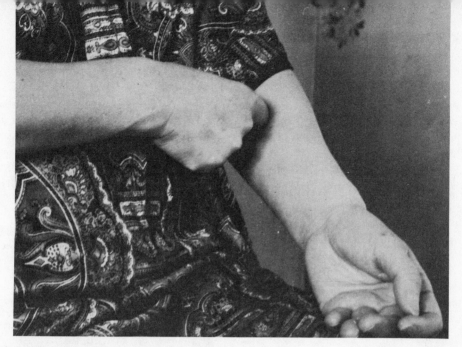

Fig. 2 - 15. Application of the middle knuckle
of the forefinger to the inside of the forearm.

Fig. 2 - 16. Application of the middle knuckle
of the forefinger to the oblique muscles of the
lower back.

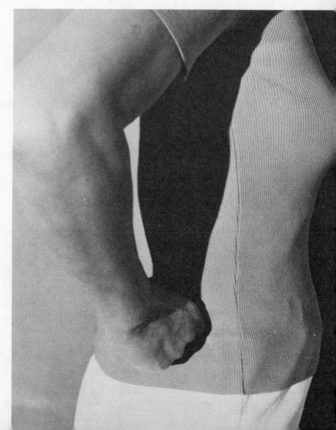

Now, to complete the use of the hands, close your fist and notice the first row of knuckles. (See Figure 2-17.)

This treatment is recommended for those who do a great deal of driving. I developed this technique myself when commuting between Palm Springs and Los Angeles, California. To my delight, I found that the fatigue and muscle strain were reduced by as much as 90 percent.

The first row of knuckles are used along the spine by sitting back against the knuckles or lying on them in bed or on the floor. This is ideal for the upper, middle, and lower back. (See Figure 2-18.)

You are now ready to practice. Chapter Two discusses the proper techniques in the use of the fingers and knuckles. Certainly, you are encouraged to read on, but before proceeding with your practice treatments, it is imperative that you totally develop your sensitivity of touch.

In the following chapters, the finger technique to use with each specific pain or tension will be described. Therefore, it is necessary to memorize each finger pressure so that you will automatically visualize the technique as it is described and thus avoid having to study the accompanying photo when you are performing the specific treatment.

Daily practice leads to perfection.

Fig. 2 - 17. A closed fist, showing the first row of knuckles.

Fig. 2 - 18. A closed fist shown with first row of knuckles positioned against the back.

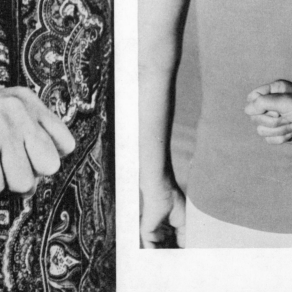

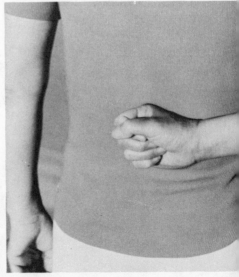

QUESTIONS
CHAPTER II

1. What is the recommended maximum thumb pressure?
   Ans. Page 19.

2. For what reason are the thumbs preferred?
   Ans. Page 20.

3. When applying pressure, what is the first tendency to avoid?
   Ans. Page 20.

4. When applying pressure what is the second most common mistake to avoid?
   Ans. Page 20.

5. What are the three steps in proper thumb application in Shiatsu?
   Ans. Page 20.

6. Besides the thumb, which finger is most frequently used for applying pressure?
   Ans. Page 22.

7. Which fingers are used in the "four finger" technique?
   Ans. Page 23.

8. Which are the most effective forearm applications?
   Review Page 21, Figure 2-3.

9. What technique is best for the abdominal area?
   Ans. Page 23, Figure 2-8.

10. What technique is best for the upperarm area?
    Ans. Page 25, Figure 2-11.

11. Name the key areas for the "middle knuckle" of the forefinger application.
    Ans. Page 26; Review Figures 2-13 thru 2-16 (Pages 26-27).

12. When and how are the "closed fist" first row of knuckles used?
    Ans. Page 28; Review Figures 2-17 and 2-18.

13. Another four finger key area technique is the upper shoulder area. Demonstrate technique-application.

    Ans. Page 25; Review Figure 2-12 (Page 25).

14. A "two-finger" application is used ,when one finger acts as a "rein-forcement" to the other. To which two fingers do we refer? and How are they used?

    Ans. Page 22; Review Figure 2-6 (Page 22).

15. Name the two best areas suited for practicing thumb pressure.

    Ans. Page 21.

CHAPTER THREE

HEADACHES

There are four particularly common types of headaches we will discuss in this chapter, along with the proper Shiatsu technique to be performed for each. As each headache is described, a sketch will be indicated to show the areas most usually afflicted by the pain.

Note: when a headache persists, this may be a symptom of a more serious organic breakdown and should not be ignored.

Arthritis Headache
The arthritis headache is a low threshold, nagging type of pain, covering some widely divergent parts of the head, neck, and shoulders, as shown in Figure 3-1.

It should be noted that arthritis headaches are usually affected by weather changes and sometimes precede the weather by as much as four or five days.

The first indication may be a stiff neck and dull headache upon arising in the morning; or occasionally, during the middle of the night, you may awaken with the back of your head pressing into the pillow and the neck arched. As a rule, the pain starts at

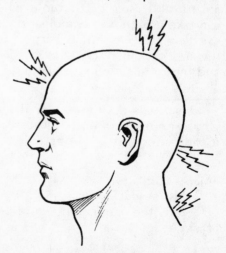

Fig. 3 - 1. Arthritis headache area.

the back of the head in the *occipital* area and radiates over the top of the head. This is exemplified in Figure 3-1.

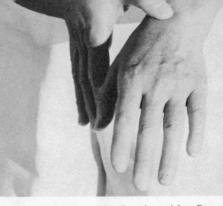

Fig. 3 - 2. Applying the thumb and forefinger on parts 1 and 2 (Figure 2 - 2).

Not all arthritis headaches start in exactly this way, but by noting the involved areas and observing the progress and pattern of these headaches, it becomes fairly simple to define the problem.

Arthritis headaches respond well to aspirin, although this relief is usually only temporary. The proper use of Shiatsu may delay the effects for days or weeks. It should be made quite clear here that Shiatsu does not eliminate the excess calcium, the cause of *osteoarthritis;* however, *rheumatoid* and *migratory arthritis* pains do respond to Shiatsu treatment. (In the case of osteoarthritis, the cause is not eliminated, but the ligaments and muscles are loosened and circulation is improved, thus providing relief for a period of time.)

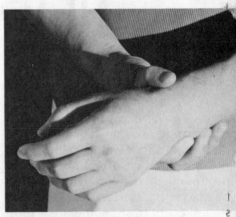

Fig. 3 - 3. Applying pressure to point 3, as shown in Figure 2 - 2.

Let us digress here for a moment and discuss the combination of Shiatsu and aspirin. For those who can take aspirin, the combination is excellent. The aspirin is carried to the area of pain much more rapidly, and the results are longer lasting.

Fig. 3 - 4. Applying pressure to points 1 and as shown in Figure 2 - 3.

Shiatsu is a Godsend to those who cannot take aspirin because of its side effects. It will bring relief.

Shiatsu Points for Arthritis Headaches

Study the diagram in Figure 2-2 carefully.

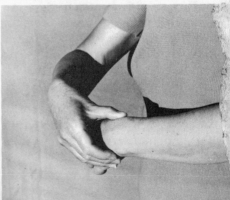

Start with the left wrist as shown in the diagram in Figure 2-2 and apply the thumb of the right hand to point 1, and the forefinger to point 2. Squeeze and hold for ten seconds. Point 3 should be applied with the thumb while holding the wrist flat on a table. (See Figures 3-2 and 3-3.) The procedure is reversed for the right arm.

The next step uses the forearms by following the points in the diagram shown in Figure 2-3.

The right hand is placed over the left wrist with the thumb on point 1 and the forefinger on point 7. (See Figure 3-4.)

Apply pressure equally on both points 2 and 7 at the same time, and hold for ten seconds; then proceed to points 2 and 8, holding for ten seconds. Proceed to points 6 and 12. It is usually good to repeat these procedures two or three times.

Now we come to the upper arm shown in the diagram in Figure 3-

The same procedure is to be followed here as with the forearm. Starting with the thumb on point 13 and the forefinger on point 17. Proceed up the arm using all points to the *deltoid* muscle, shown at point 20, and the thumb at point 16 (which is one of the critical *neurovascular* areas). Great caution should be exercised at both points 15 and 16.

We will now concentrate our efforts on the neck *(cervical)* region. Most arthritis headaches start in this area because of calcium *spurs* forming along the *vertebrae* (neck/spine bones). These spurs, very much like the spur on a chicken's leg, strike the nerves that lie between the vertebrae, sending waves of pain over the head and down the arm. If the spur lies between the *atlas* and *first cervical vertabra,* it will produce a dull, bruising pain behind the eyes, as though someone were pounding the eyeball. All of these affected areas are shown in Figure 3-1.

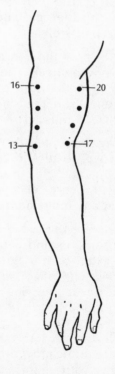

Fig. 3 - 5. Points of pressure on the upper arm. (Pressure: ten pounds.)

The previous discussion of the physical cause of arthritis headaches is as much as western medicine knows about the cause of arthritis.

We shall now discuss the Oriental philosophy related to the cause of arthritis.

To begin with, let us refer to the Yin and Yang syndrome. We are all creatures of conditioning for every action, except the *autonomic reflex* actions. Actually, even these are altered by conditioning, to some degree.

We now have a Yin and Yang situation between muscle groups, with the *cerebral cortex* (the communication center of the brain) supplying the energy and maintaining the balance.

You ask how this has an effect on arthritis of the neck. The primary irritant is in the passing of a conditioned reflex from the brain to certain nerves and muscles.

Leverage muscles are members of either the extensor or flexor group. Your muscles must work together with a very delicate balance to perform any movement.

To describe the function of extensor muscles, extend your fingers out—the extensor muscles are the prime movers. (A slight opposition from the flexor muscles keeps a smooth motion.)

The flexor muscles in the above situation are prime movers in closing the fingers, with slight opposition from the extensor muscles.

You now have a very basic idea of how locomotor nerves are activated. Let us assume that you are a golfer playing several times a month and all of a sudden you decide to improve your game. Advice is offered by many people and soon you become confused and frustrated. If you continue to play for a long period, in this confused and frustrated state, you will develop a chronic tension. Depending on inherent weakness, this chronic tension will manifest itself anywhere from your wrist to your lower back. It is then that a chronic fibrosis will develop and these wire-like tissues will eventually become arthritic. This sequence of frustration and pressure over a continued period of time are the negative and positive or Yang and Yin syndromes.

The syndromes may result from marriage, work, sports, childhood pressures, or almost anything that is constant and repetitious.

I have digressed long enough so let us return to the neck points as shown in the diagram in Figure 3-6.

The points 1 through 12 are reached in a very simple manner. (See Figure 3-7.) With fingers locked together, thumbs extending down, place the right thumb on point 2 and the left thumb on point 1 and then move through *all twelve points*. Repeat this two or three times.

This exercise will bring blood to the nerves and vertebrae and relax the muscles and ligaments. It will also help stimulate the cortex (control center).

The above are the key points for the arthritis headache.

In order to clarify various head pains, a general category is referred to as an arthritis headache. The cause of the pain may originate anywhere in the body, but the discomfort (or pain) will be noticed in the head.

Note: There is actually an arthritis headache in which calcium forms in lumps on top of the head. However, this is very unusual and ordinarily is not as painful as the so-called arthritis headache.

Combining Shiatsu with standard medical treatment, i.e., aspirin, is very beneficial and creates no conflict. By reducing muscle tension and increasing circulation Shiatsu actually improves the body's assimilation.

Fig. 3 - 7. Applying pressure to points 1 - 12 (Figure 3 - 6) with finger locked and thumbs extending down.

Sinus Headache

The sinus headache is an extremely complicated headache with variable types of symptoms and contributory causes. Unlike the arthritis headache, the sinus headache has no stationary or permanent source or irritation.

To oversimplify, a collection of waste material (or mucus) in the sinus cavities creates a pressure on the nerves in the sinus areas.

Therefore, a "shotgun" approach must be taken to cover all of the sinus areas, including the nerves on the top of the head and the back (or occipital) area.

(For reference, see the diagrams in Figures 3-6 and 3-8, 3-9, 3-11.)

The sinus cavities are, of course, the culprits, and the pain is generally a surface pain around the eyes. There is occasional deep pain immediately behind the eye, caused by an acute infection of the sinus

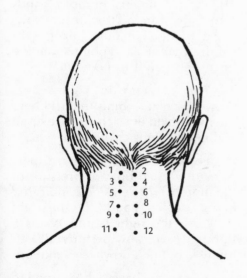

Fig. 3 - 6. Pressure points in the neck. (Pressure: twelve pounds.)

cavities adjacent to the eye which spreads inflammation to the orbital eye muscles.

Some of the more uncommon areas that may become irritated are the back of the head, or occipital area, the parotid gland area, under the jaw and below the ear, and the temporal area, the side of the head in front of the ear. The latter is the most common because of its proximity to the sinus cavities above and below the eyes.

Shiatsu Points for Sinus Headaches

Study the diagram in Figure 3-8 carefully, indicating each side of nostril.

Use both forefingers for point 1 and point 2, press at a 45 degree angle, and hold for ten seconds.

To be certain you have struck the correct points, you will feel a dull spreading pain extending up along the nose and around the eyes. This will then be followed by a *clearing* or relaxing sensation. It may take a little practice until you strike the exact trigger points.

The diagram in Figure 3-9 indicates the four pressure points around each eye. Press the lower points, points 1, 2, 5, and 6, with the forefingers. Press the points above the eye (points 3, 4, 7, and 8) with the thumbs.

The diagram in Figure 3-10 shows the top of the head. Press points 1 through 6 with the middle finger of each hand, using both hands simultaneously. This exercise will help relieve sinuses, neck,

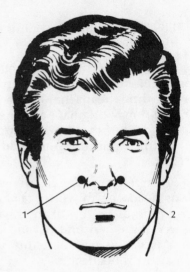

Fig. 3 - 8. Pressure points for a sinus headache. (Pressure: ten pounds.)

shoulders, and upper back.
The next diagram (Figure 3-11) is a variation of Figure 3-10.

Place (as indicated in Figure 3-11) all five fingers of both hands across the top of the head. Now, move point 7 (middle finger right hand) to point 8 and point 9 (middle finger left hand) to point 10.

The diagram in Figure 3-12 shows the eight points that will help the throat and eustachian tube drain and empty sinus cavities.

Points 1 through 4 are performed with an upward pressure of the thumb. *(The left side is indicated here;* use left hand; for the right side, use the right hand.) Points 5 through 8 are also performed with thumbs, but in a downward motion.

Points may have to be probed to locate the nerve in a soft mass at the lower corner of the jawbone. Points

5 through 8 are on the backside of the *sternomastoid*, located along the cord at the side of the neck.

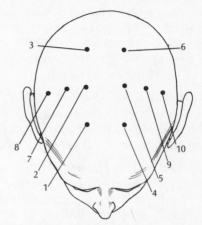

Fig. 3 - 11. Pressure points of the top of the head, a variation of Figure 3 - 10. (Pressure: ten pounds.)

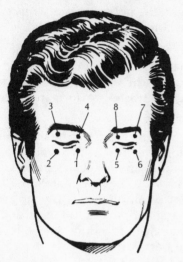

Fig. 3 - 9. Pressure points around the eyes. (Pressure: ten pounds.)

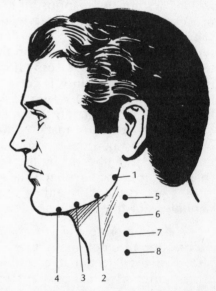

Fig. 3 - 12. Pressure points of the throat and eustauhian tube. (Pressure Ten Pounds.)

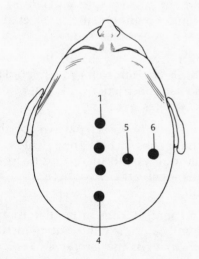

ig. 3 - 10. Pressure points of the top of the ead. (Pressure: ten pounds.)

The object in working the preceding points for the sinus headache is to promote drainage of the sinus cavities and thus relieve the pressure.

The exact cause of the sinus headache is still not known. The first and most commonly accepted cause is inherent allergy; the more recent is of psychosomatic origin.

I have developed a theory of my own which is a composite of these two and also provides a reasonable explanation for the common cold.

The first theory (inherent allergy) suggests that a person is born with a tendency toward sinus problems and that pollen, dust, or some other irritant triggers the sinus.

If this tendency is inherited, which system is responsible? A process of elimination will leave only the respiratory and the nervous systems, or a combination of the two. Therefore, if it is respiratory, then the existing theory is correct; but if it is the nervous system, we have a direct connection to the second theory (psychosomatic). Thus, we now have a neuropsychosomatic condition, strengthened by the fact that no appreciable bacteria or viruses are present in either sinus conditions or the common cold.

The common cold will invariably occur after an emotional crisis. It is also a medical fact that emotional stress and physical exhaustion produce *lactic acid* in the nervous system. The common cold acts as a safety reaction, flushing the nervous system and thus preventing permanent damage to neural conduction. Further evidence supporting this theory is that milk is high in lactic acid and is mucus forming; people with colds and sinus conditions are advised not to drink milk.

The sinus condition being inherent means the individual has a chronic emotional insecurity and when the body begins to relax at night, the nervous system reacts with flushing.

Shiatsu is of great benefit by relaxing the muscles around the areas of the sinus cavities thus relieving the waste-pressure and allowing drainage.

There is a great deal of current scientific research available, including the McGill Studies, that leads us to believe that over 70 percent of all disease is psychosomatic in origin. Both physiological and psychological reactions are effects of the nervous system.

Tension Headaches

The tension headache may be the preexisting condition for all other headaches. These are more frequent in the young, and if left as a chronic condition, they will evolve into more serious traumas.

It is also my belief that these chronic conditions may be related to vascular constrictions, hypertension, i.e., strokes, etc.

There is no set pattern for the tension headache. They will vary from one eye to the entire head or one small area anywhere on the skull.

There is one area that is apparently a prime contributing factor, and that is the serratus posticus superior muscle (Figure 3-13).

The serratus posticus superior muscle connects to the lower neck vertebrae and the upper back vertebrae, functioning as a stabilizer; the same muscle, on the opposite side, acts as a counterbalance.

The serratus muscles in conjunction with rhomboideus (minor) put a tremendous strain on the upper back (dorsal), middle and lower neck (cervical) vertebrae; this results in tension headaches with occasional shoulder involvement. Figure 3-14 shows how the rhomboidei pull on the vertebrae.

The levator anguli scapulae is the secondary contributing factor and is illustrated in Figure 3-15. This is the muscle used in raising the arm; and the resultant action is a contrary force to the primary groups of muscle.

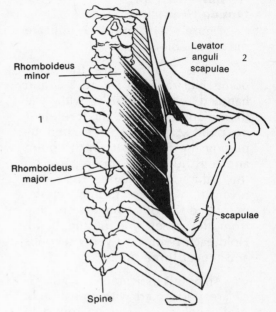

Fig. 3 - 14. The rhomboidei muscles pulling on the vertebra.

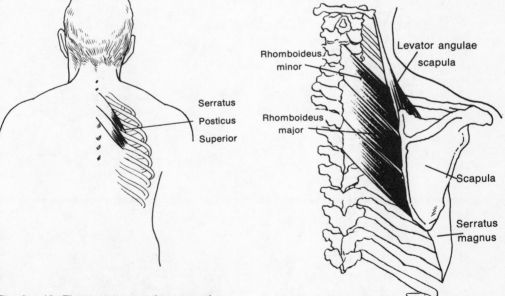

Fig. 3 - 13. The serratus posticus superior muscle, which connects the lower neck and upper back vertebrae.

Fig. 3 - 15. The levator angulae scapula.

Pressure Points for Tension Headaches

Figures 3-16 and 3-17 indicate the relief points.

Points 1 and 2 are the same points illustrated in Figure 2-2, and handled simultaneously with the thumb on point 1 and the forefinger on point 2. Point 3 is reached by placing the forefinger on the point and the thumb pressing against on the palm of the hand. Point 4 is reversed, with the thumb on the point and the other fingers pressing from the other side of the hand. Hold each point for twenty seconds and repeat three times.

All points indicated on Figure 3-17 are performed with the thumb. Additional points can be found in Figure 3-5. Follow the instructions for that figure. The diagram in Figure 3-6 will be of help; and using the diagrams in Figures 3-11 and 3-12 will be beneficial to these tension headaches.

Migraine Headache

The migraine headache symptoms range from nausea to abdominal and head pains, with visions being disturbed by auras around objects. There appears to be a connection between the pyloric nerves of the stomach, the radial and ulnar nerves of the arm, and the trigemenal and sinus nerves of the face and head.

There is undoubtedly an emotional trigger, but the cause of the migraine is the most mysterious and least understood of all headaches; no positive link has been established.

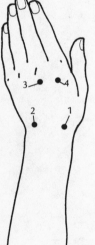

Fig. 3 - 16. The four pressure points on the hand for relief of tension headaches. (Pressure: ten pounds.)

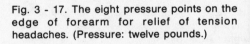

Fig. 3 - 17. The eight pressure points on the edge of forearm for relief of tension headaches. (Pressure: twelve pounds.)

In my work, I have found a connection between the pyloric plexus of the stomach and the radial and ulnar nerves of the arms. That is why pressure points in the arm are used in conjunction with the abdominal pressure points. The femoral nerve of the thigh is another related area, along with the tibial, the peroneal, and the popliteal of the lower leg.

All four points indicated in Figure 3-18 are done with the middle finger, plus a very light pressure from the forefinger and ring (third) finger.

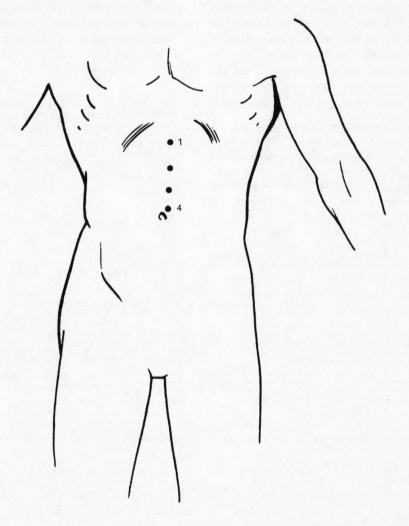

Fig. 3 - 18. Four key pressure points for the pyloric nerves. (Pressure: ten pounds.)

All ten points shown in Figure 3-19 are done with the middle finger plus a very light pressure from the forefinger and ring (third) finger.

Exercise Pressure Points for Migraine Headaches

The diagrams in Figures 2-2 and 2-3 are a good starting place for the arm pressure points. Follow this procedure (the method shown in Figure 3-5), particularly on points 11 through 15. The diagram in Figure 3-6 is also valuable (follow as directed), and of course as just explained, those shown in Figures 3-17 and 3-18.

This concludes the chapter on the four most common headaches. We have covered theoretical causes and the self-application of Shiatsu pressure points for the relief of these ailments.

When modern medicine becomes more aware of this ancient art, there will be more studies performed with astounding proven theories and no doubt many spin-offs bringing us full circle back to the simple and basic arts.

There are always unknown factors involved, and they exist in everything; however, the results of the pressure techniques are irrefutable.

Note: It is always important to remember that a headache can be a symptom of a more serious problem and should a headache persist, always contact qualified medical assistance.

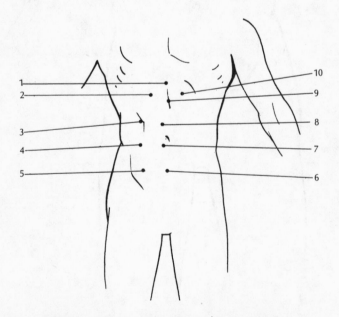

Fig. 3 - 19. The ten pressure points of the general gastro intestinal area. (Pressure: ten pounds.)

QUESTIONS
CHAPTER III

1. Name the two common arthritis headache symptoms.
   Ans. Page 31.

2. Shiatsu does not eliminate osteo-arthritis; however, relief for a period of time is noticed with this exercise. Why?
   Ans. Page 32.

3. Diagram I indicates the Shiatsu Points For Arthritis Headaches. What is the pressure you are to use?
   Ans. Pages 32-33.

4. Diagram II indicates pressure points on the forearm. Demonstrate which two fingers are used.
   Ans. Page 32; Review Figure 3-2 (Page 32); Figure 3-3 (Page 32).

5. What may a dull, bruising pain behind the eyes indicate?
   Ans. Page 33.

6. Review Figure 3-5, Page 33 and indicate which finger is on the deltoid muscle (Point 20)?
   Ans. Page 33, Figure 3-5 (Page 33).

7. What is the "Cerebral Cortex" and what is its function?
   Ans. Page 34.

8. Figure 3-4 (Page 32) indicates Shiatsu Points for the Neck. What is the pressure you are to use?
   Ans. Page 35, Figure 3-6.

9. How many pressure points are indicated on the Neck?
   Ans. Figure 3-6. Page 35.

10. You should never take medication with Shiatsu. True or False?
    Ans. Page 35.

11. What is the "shotgun" approach relative to Sinus headaches?

    Ans. Page 35.

12. Diagram V indicates Shiatsu Points for sinus headache at nostril. What is the pressure to be used?

    Ans. Review Figure 3-8 (Page 36).

13. Figure 3-9 indicates pressure points around each eye. How many are indicated?

    Ans. Page 36.

14. What technique is used to locate the nerve in a soft mass at the lower corner of the jawbone?

    Ans. Pages 36-37.

15. There is no set pattern for the tension headache. There is however, a prime contributing muscle. Name it.

    Ans. Page 38.

16. The serratus muscles combine with which muscle to effect a tremendous strain on the upper back, middle and lower neck?

    Ans. Page 39.

17. Figure 3-15, Page 39, indicates the "Levator Anguli" muscle. Name its function.

    Ans. Page 39.

CHAPTER FOUR
NECK and SHOULDERS

This chapter will have five segments: cervical arthritis; rheumatoid arthritis; osteoporosis; cervical disc or vertebral deterioration; and bruises. Each segment will be devoted to an explanation of why each disorder develops and the points of pressure used to relieve it.

Probably, the most frequent area for pain is the neck, and rightly so, because of its delicate nature and its vulnerability to shock and strain. The vertebrae of the neck have very delicate ligaments and muscles in order to permit mobility. Interestingly enough, as we age, the neck is the first area to lose its elasticity and start calcifying. We know this progressive deterioration occurs, but there is a great lack of knowledge about the contributing factors.

The contributing factors contain vital information that I have been observing for the past twenty years. The relation of contributing factors to the hemiated disc will be discussed in this chapter.

Similarities appear between this chapter and sections of Chapter three. Cervical arthritis is one disorder that may assume a pain in either the head, spine, shoulder, arm, or hand. Another section which has a great deal in common with the preceding chapter section on tension headaches will be found here in the section on the emotional stress syndrome.

The emotional variables that contribute to cervical arthritis will be observed in greater depth and we shall see how the same disease may be manifested by different symptoms. It is also possible that occupational stress syndromes and arthritis are connected. We will note the emotional patterns of those prone to arthritis.

By the end of this chapter the five divided segments will dovetail into one, and even bruises will evidence a kinship.

Cervical Arthritis

To provide a visual understanding of cervical arthritis, carefully examine the illustration in Figure 4-1. At point x there is a calcium deposit, located between the third and fourth cervical vertebra. Now, it is not just the calcium that causes the pain, but the pressure the calcium places on the nerve that lies between the vertebrae.

The nerve located between the second and third cervical vertebra has its effect on two separate and unrelated areas. A most commonly affected area is the arm, where the nerve extends down the body and may carry the pain along the nerves trunk. Another area of pain is in the area of the sympathetic nerve ending in the throat. The sympathetic nerve may also, upon rare occasion, produce fever.

Arthritis on different vertebrae will have vastly different effects. For instance, should there be a deposit on the first and third cervical vertebrae, you might have a sympathetic pain carried to the back of the eyeball (as described in the section on arthritis headache). A deposit on the fourth cervical vertebra may have an effect on the circulation of the upper body. The ones we are particularly concerned with here are the seventh cervical vertebra and the first dorsal vertebra because they affect the shoulders and arms.

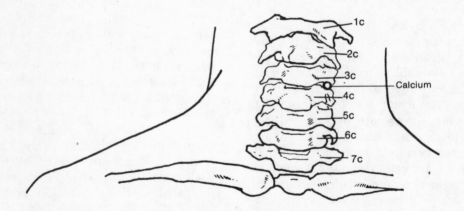

Fig. 4 - 1. Vertebra shown with calcium deposits. These are formed like coral.

Psychosomatic origin is a possible cause, as discussed previously, of arthritis headache; this is also true of arthritis of the neck. Chronic tension and anxiety contribute to arthritis of the neck. How or where the calcium deposits come from, no one seems to know exactly, but there is strong evidence that links either the kidney or lower gastrointestinal tract, or both, as a part of the cause. An overactivity of the pyloric nerves, which control the neural complex of the visceral (stomach and gastrointestinal tract) organs, appears to stimulate the production of calcium deposits.

There seems to be a personality type that is arthritis prone. This person is usually introverted, self-critical, and a perfectionist.

Arthritis may be triggered by injuries or shock. There are many documented cases, particularly of women who have tragically lost a child and who then develop rheumatoid arthritis overnight.

To be more specific, rheumatoid arthritis is primarily an inflammation of the soft tissue over the joint and has no calcium deposits. It can therefore develop overnight. In osteoarthritis calcium deposits are building up slowly for years. It is important to understand these two basic types of arthritis; many other types are variations of these two.

A third type of arthritis is a deterioration of the bone; this is called osteoporosis.

Let us summarize the two major types of arthritis along with their psychosomatic sources.

Rheumatoid arthritis is characterized by inflammation. The appearance is very sudden and usually strikes several areas or the entire body. The pain is excruciating and the area is extremely sensitive to touch. The onset of the disease is frequently preceded by an emotional trauma, and the disease is more common among women than men. The personality that is prone to this type of arthritis is one that places a great deal of himself into anything he believes in and has difficulty accepting failure.

Osteoporosis is a honeycombing of the bone. The bone becomes porous, loses most of its elasticity, and has a tendency to break. Osteoporosis is also more common among women and usually develops after menopause. This might indicate a hormone deficiency. It is interesting to note that women most frequently develop osteoporosis of the third cervical vertebra, which has a relationship to several respiratory areas. Fever is also common in this type of condition. It is possible that acute emotional trauma is a cause factor.

A very common area for manifestation of osteoporosis is the hip joint, and this condition seems to be more common in men. There is a strong organic and muscular connection to the hips through the lower lumbar and upper sacral nerve ends in the spine. These nerve ends are connected to the reproductive organs, which may or may not produce a hormone change in the lower trunk.

Osteo arthritis - calcium forms near the nerve trunks or ganglia among the vertebrae or joint. This type of arthritis takes years to form and is frequently related to childhood emotional trauma, marital unhappiness or occupational pressure. This person can tend to fall into the whipping boy class.

Cervical Arthritis Pressure Points

These pressure points apply for all three types of arthritis. However, please note that you should use less pressure for rheumatoid and osteoporosis types.

In rheumatoid arthritis, the affected area is usually so sensitive that it is sometimes advisable to work only the extremities until the sensitivity of the cervical area decreases. The first pressure in the cervical vertebrae should not be more than three or four pounds.

The danger with osteoporosis is that if too much pressure is applied, the bone will shatter.

The related areas that are not affected by osteoporosis may take the recommended pressures.

Refer again to the diagram in Figure 2-3. and follow the same procedure. In some unusual cases of rheumatoid arthritis, there may be inflammation of the wrist. If so, extreme caution should be exercised.

The diagram in Figure 4-2 differs from the forearm directions for arthritis headache and should be followed carefully.

Pressure points 1 through 5, as shown in the diagram, as well as those in the diagram in Figure 2-2, have an effect on the large intestine and its sphere of influence. This has a relationship to all types of arthritis. Pressure should be applied with the thumb and pressing down. (See Figure 4-3.)

The diagram in Figure 4-4 is also a part of this application (called *tsubo*) to the upper arm area. Pressure is applied with the forefinger as shown in Figure 4-5.

The diagram in Figure 4-6 shows the *tsubo* points for the small and large intestines. Start with pressure point 1 and follow through point 16. *Hold each point for twenty seconds* using the middle finger.

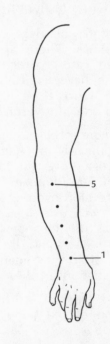

Fig. 4 - 2. Pressure points of the forearm. (Pressure: twelve pounds.)

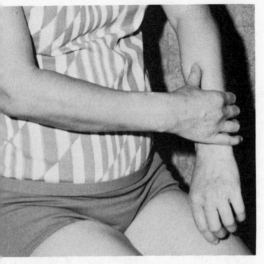

Fig. 4 - 3. Applying the thumb to the pressure points of the forearm.

Fig. 4 - 4. Pressure points on upper arm area. (Pressure: twelve pounds.)

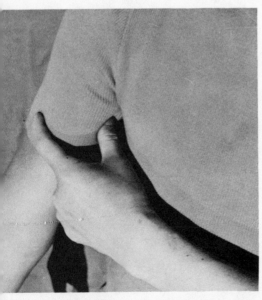

Fig. 4 - 5. Application of pressure on upper arm with forefinger.

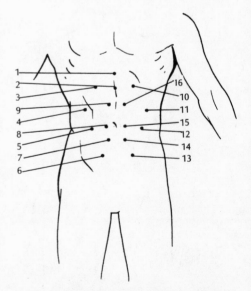

Fig. 4 - 6. *Tsubo* points for small and large intestines. (Pressure: ten pounds.)

As an exercise, refer to instructions for sinus headaches and follow the same directions, using the same pressure indicated for Figures 3-6, 3-10, and 3-12.

Now, use the diagram in Figure 4-7, to show how to apply pressure to a point not previously shown, but which might be used for a tension headache too.

This is an exception for the use of the fourfinger technique (shown in Figure 2-8), and is accomplished by reaching across with the right arm to the left side, and vice versa.

The scapula group work as elevators for raising the arms and moving the shoulders.

We have now covered the key points for arthritis of the neck and should have established some degree of relief through application of these instructions. There is one unusual feature that will sometimes occur with Shiatsu: it will, in some cases, require twenty-four hours or more after application to note the effects or results. Years of observation have led me to believe that circulation and blood pressure are the determining factors in this delay. The lower the pressure, the longer the time period needed to note the results. With osteoarthritis, I feel that calcium deposits may be a secondary factor.

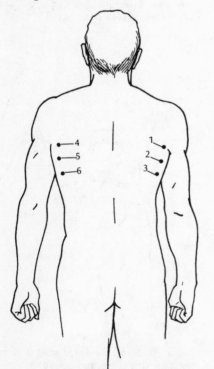

Fig. 4 - 7. Pressure points of shoulder group (Scapula). (Pressure: twelve pounds.)

Cervical Disc or Vertebrae Deterioration

Cervical disc or vertebrae deterioration is a very common cause of neck and shoulder pains. The cerivcal disc or vertebrae deterioration is difficult, but not impossible, to treat.

Between each vertebra we have a disc or cushion. Because of chronic strain or injury, these discs sometimes herniate or deteriorate, allowing the vertebrae above and below the affected area to come together and pinch the nerve that lies between them.

How do we develop disc herniation? Most generally the herniation is from prolonged tension; however an injury where the vertebrae are driven together, such as in a fall, will also cause this herniation. It is not unusual for these injuries to manifest themselves many years after the original injury. Study the following illustrations (Figures 4-8 and 4-9.)

You will observe that the disc has collapsed permitting the two vertebrae to come together with the second vertebra tilting up, on the right side.

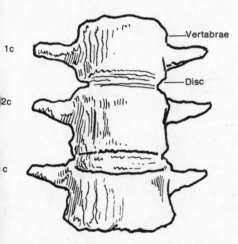

Fig. 4 - 8. Normal vertebra and discs.

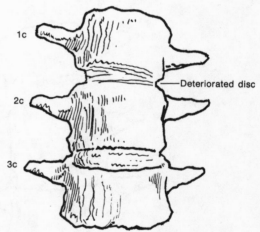

Fig. 4 - 9. A damaged or deteriorated disc that has collapsed causing pressure on the first cervical nerve.

In some cases it is not the disc but the vertebra itself that has been wearing, as shown in Figure 4-10. This deterioration is sometimes due to osteoporosis, but may be nothing more than wear. The deterioration in the second vertebra causes the third vertebra to tilt up.

Vertebra deterioration will eventually start a Christmas-tree-effect upon many vertebrae, above and below, by throwing them to the side and creating pressure on the various nerves. The guide muscles along the wing of each vertebra attempt to compensate for the strain, but in so doing, it will usually create related muscle strains that must be released after a time.

The first thing to ascertain is whether you have a vertebra protruding to one side or the other. To be sure it is a vertebra and not calcium, run your thumb around the area and determine whether it is cartilaginous or osseous (calcium, bony). Cartilage will have a plastic texture and will be a bit softer. Calcium will be the consistency of coral, with rather sharp edges. Both the cervical disc and vertebra deterioration will have almost the same consistency.

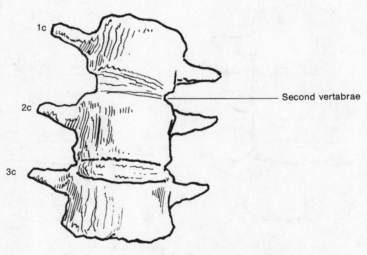

Fig. 4 - 10. Deterioration in second vertebra, causing vertebra to drop and pinch first cervical nerve.

Having determined whether it is the disc or vertebra, follow these points. Refer to the diagram in Figure 2-3 and follow all ten points, as suggested. Now, go on to the diagram in Figure 3-5 and follow the instruction given for this. The next diagram (Figure 4-11) is different from the others and is reached by turning the hand as shown in Figure 4-12. Use this technique on both sides of the head.

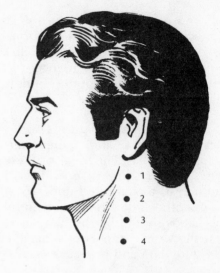

Fig. 4 - 11. Pressure points along the side of the neck. (Pressure: ten pounds.)

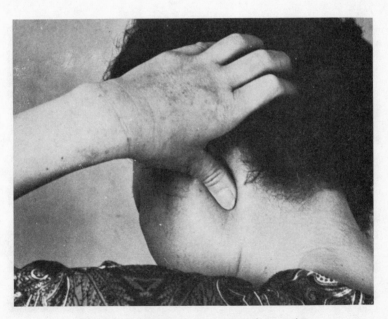

Fig. 4 - 12. Applying pressure to points on the side of the neck. Press inward with the thumb.

The next diagram (Figure 4-13) shows how to relieve the occipital (back of the head) area. Follow points 1 through 6 in sequence after studying the position of the hands in Figure 4-14.

The diagram in Figure 4-15 indicates the jaw and upper sternomastoid areas. For relief of these areas follow pressure points 1 through 3, as indicated and repeat on the other side. The placement of the hands should be the same as in that shown in the previous diagram in Figure 4-13 and in Figure 4-14.

We have now covered the main problems in and exercises related to cervical disc and vertebral deteriorations.

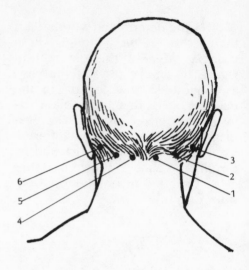

Fig. 4 - 13. Pressure points around head area. (Pressure: twelve pounds.)

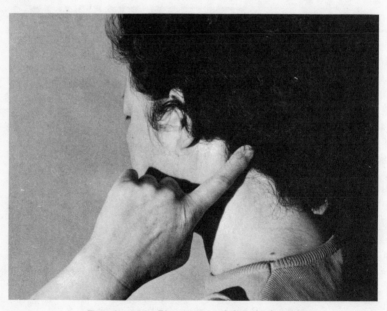

Fig. 4 - 14. Placement of hands in using pressure points shown in Figure 4 - 13. The forefinger is used for pressure.

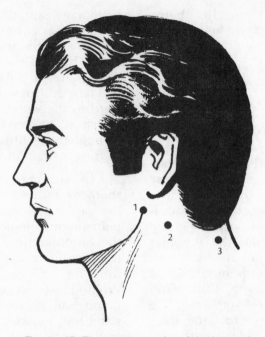

Fig. 4 - 15. The pressure point of the jaw and upper sternoid areas. (Pressure: ten pounds.)

Occupational Strain

Occupational strain may actually be the predecessor of the cervical disc and vertebral deterioration. Arthritis and vertebral deterioration, in many cases, are the result of what we call occupational strain. If Shiatsu is utilized early in its development, it is possible to prevent, or at least greatly minimize, the effects of occupational strain.

Early indications of occupational strain will usually manifest themselves at the end of a day's work, or sometimes they will start during the course of the day. In the very early stages, the condition may appear to be nothing more than a slight stiffness or a minor headache that usually passes barely noticed.

This type of pain or stiffness should not be confused with that derived from physically hard labor performed occasionally. Occupational strain is caused by a repetitious motion and, interestingly enough, has a psychosomatic origin that may be because of the pressure of a job. Strain symptoms do not necessarily occur immediately and it therefore is difficult to establish the cause.

I was quite surprised to learn that many people coming to me for treatment had actually been told by their supervisors to seek new employment. This may not only prolong this problem, but can create many new ones; there are other and much better solutions. The solution I would recommend, of course, is found in Shiatsu, another being professional psychiatric help.

Assuming you have selected Shiatsu, the first step is to locate the area of distress. Having done this, the next step is to ascertain exactly what motion you perform in your job is causing the symptom. A typical example could be a secretarial job requiring typing. The physical strain originates in the hands and because of the difficulty of holding the shoulders erect, where the strain is picked up by the scapula group (muscles lying under the shoulder blades), which in turn involve the infraspinatus and the rhomboidei that connect to the fourth, fifth, sixth, and seventh cervical vertebrae. The rhomboidei angle across the back where they interrelate with the scapula muscles. Because the rhomboidei are connected with the scapula group or elevators, they will be affected by chronic strain from that area and should a condition become chronic, it will eventually produce spasms in the rhomboidei. This will then reflect on the

vertebrae, causing a slight dislocation, or a compression of the vertebrae or the spinal nerves of the area. This also has an influence on the elevator anguli scapula (a muscle that angles from the shoulder upward to the vertebrae of the neck), which is connected to the first through the fourth cervical vertebra, causing a strain in that area.

In summary then, chronic shoulder and arm tension may, under prolonged conditions, cause a permanent compression of any of the vertebrae from the first cervical through the fourth thoracic, depending on congenital weakness. It should be stated here that this condition will occur only where the stabilizing muscles are weak, or as with modern man, underdeveloped. I have added the following illustrations so you may better visualize the process through the two groups of muscles and how the scapula group is related to the shoulder girdle group. (See Figures 4-16 and 4-17.)

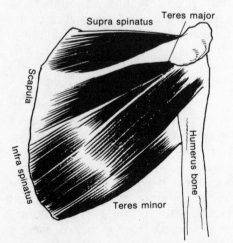

Fig. 4 - 16. The scapula group of bones.

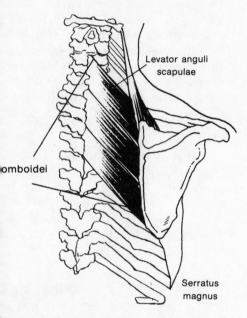

Levator anguli
scapulae

omboidei

Serratus
magnus

Fig. 4 - 17. The shoulder girdle group of
bones.

There are other contributing
actors to chronic shoulder and arm
ension that is also related to the
ower back, which will be discussed
n a later chapter.

It is of the utmost importance to
be able to analyze your symptoms
and their cause in order to better
provide the proper treatment area
or correction and relief.

Approximately 90 percent of the
houlder and neck problems start in
he scapular muscles, and I will start
with that area in the next diagram
Figure 4-18).

Fig. 4 - 18. The scapular ring, covering the key
muscles. (Pressure: twelve pounds.)

In order to reach the twelve pressure points indicated in Figure 4-18, study each of the photographs in Figures 4-19 and 4-20 carefully. Finding these points will require practice

Points 1 through 5, follow Figure 4-19.

For points 6 through 12, the middle finger is used, as shown in Figure 4-20. It is possible to use the four-finger pressure, but the middle finger is preferable.

To locate points 10 through 12, find the outer and upper edge of the scapula and come directly across and slightly up (toward the neck). You may want to use a mirror to help in locating these points. Remember the right side is done with the left hand. Figure 3-6 should also be included as an exercise with the pressures indicated.

This covers the prime areas for relief of occupational strain. The procedures mentioned should be repeated once or twice daily for one week, even though the symptoms may subside after the first or second application.

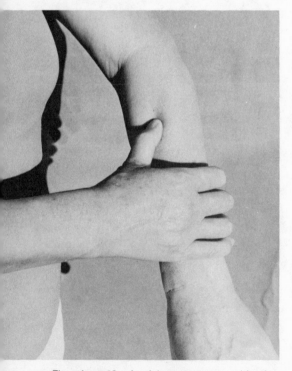

Fig. 4 - 19. Applying pressure with the knuckles.

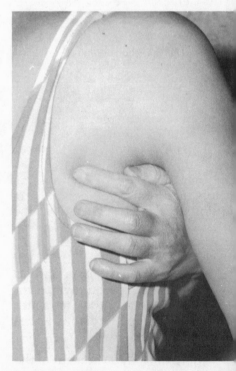

Fig. 4 - 20. Reaching under the arm to apply pressure to the teres muscles.

EMOTIONAL STRESS

Chronic tension is the basic cause of cervical arthritis, occupational strain, cervical disc or vertebra deterioration, and emotional stress.

Let me show you some examples of an occu-emotional stress situation: A conscientious person is working in a highly-skilled position, but this person is insecure. He has a supervisor who is domineering and, of course, relentless in his criticism of those he is supervising. Yet, the supervisor is less capable in his work skills than those he supervises. The conscientious person's resentment builds over a period of time until it becomes a neuromuscular reaction, and as time continues, more symptoms develop. This is the on-the-job stimuli.

A variation of this is the businessman who has always worked hard trying to please everyone and one day finds his business in bankruptcy. He becomes very self-critical.

Or, another example might be the corporate director who is very capable, but because of office politics suddenly finds himself out of his job. However, he is unaware of this political manipulation and feels that he is a failure. These are all examples of occu-emotional stress.

The other type of emotional stress is brought on by problems at home or by social rejection by relatives or friends.

An example might be that of a man or a woman whose mate is over-ly jealous or critical. If one person also happens to be self-critical, in most situations he or she will take the blame or assume the responsibility given for a situation. This will develop emotional stress syndromes in that person and over the years the condition will become chronic.

Be watchful of these trigger situations so that you may keep the physiological syndromes from becoming chronic and leading to a breakdown of the system. Perhaps these examples will help you to analyze your own emotional situations and their physical results.

Emotional Stress Pressure Points

Review the diagrams in Figures 4-2, 4-4, 4-6, 4-11, 4-13, and 4-15.

BRUISES

We are all familiar with the small bruises acquired in everyday living. Many small bruises go unnoticed and are of little consequence, other than being disfiguring. It is true that they can be covered with makeup, but makeup will wear off and physiologically, it is better to repair the damaged capillaries.

First, apply ice directly over the bruise for ten seconds and then remove it for another ten seconds. Repeat this procedure for approximately ten minutes.

The next step is to place a finger (preferably the forefinger) just below the bruise and press inwardly, using about *six pounds of pressure*. Hold this position for ten seconds and move to a point directly below the area, about one-half inch. Use three points, and each time move clockwise around the bruise. This will reduce about 90 percent of the swelling and discoloration.

The Bone Bruise or Deep Tissue Bruise

These bruises will not always produce discoloration, but are more painful and may continue to hurt for a very long time unless immediate action is taken.

In sports today, trainers use liquid oxygen to freeze a bruise, but this is not available to the average person and if not used properly, it might prove dangerous.

The same Shiatsu procedure described for small bruises should be followed with these exceptions. Apply the ice for a longer period—up to thirty minutes. Use about *twelve pounds of pressure* instead of six. Obviously, I cannot recommend which finger to use for the pressure; this will have to be determined by the area that is involved. This time, I will leave that to your discretion.

Neural Trunk Bruise

I have saved the most complicated bruise of all for the last. This bruise is along one of the main nerve trunks that are usually protected by bone, muscle, and ligaments. Occasionally, a bruise is received in this difficult area, and there is nothing that will last longer. Ice is of little help in this instance.

Shiatsu is worth its weight in gold in easing these bruises. Study the diagram in Figure 4-21, which indicates the bruise and how to select the pressure points. The lower limb

has been used for this diagram as it is easier to sketch.

This chapter has been dedicated primarily to the neck and shoulders, but many of the points discussed can be adjusted to fit other problems in any part of the body.

Remember, when the Shiatsu points are related to an existing condition elsewhere, then by all means use them. There are many, many more combinations that could be given here but, I prefer to simplify the process and familiarize you with only the basic techniques. If you comprehend the interrelationship between muscle groups and can correlate them with the system and Shiatsu techniques, you may wish additional information. If so, write or visit me at the Shiatsu-Thera-Center, my office, in Desert Hot Springs, California.

*"If the pain in the neck
feels like boulders,
It is always wise
to work on the shoulders"*

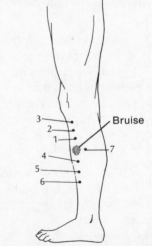

Fig. 4 - 21. A neural trunk bruise. (Pressure: twelve pounds.)

QUESTIONS
CHAPTER IV

1. Five disorders are discussed in this chapter. Name these five segments.
   Ans. Page 45.

2. Cervical arthritis may assume a pain in either of five areas, name them.
   Ans. Page 45.

3. Emotional stress syndrome is related to arthritis as well as other diseases. True or False.
   Ans. Page 45.

4. The person usually introverted, self-critical and a perfectionist is said to be a personality type who is   prone.
   Ans. Page 47.

5. What are the main differences between rheumatoid and osteo-arthritis?
   Ans. Page 47.

6. Describe "osteoporosis".
   Ans. Page 47.

7. What special rule should be observed when working with rheumatoid arthritis?
   Ans. Page 48.

8. The pressure points in Figure 4-2 (Page 49) indicating the top-side of the forearm effect an unusual area. Name it.
   Ans. Page 48.

9. The Scapula group work as elevators for raising the arms and moving the shoulders. True or False.
   Ans. Page 50.

10. How do you determine whether a deposit is from calcification or herniation?
    Ans. Page 52.

11. How many pressure points are indicated for the relief of the occipit (back of the head) area?

    Ans. Page 54. Review Figure 4-13.

12. How will occupational strain early indicate themselves?

    Ans. Page 55.

13. Which vertabrae are involved in occupational strain, as given in this Chapter?

    Ans. Page 56.

14. Where are the "Teres" muscles located?

    Ans. Review Figure 4-16 (Page 56.)

15. Explain the occu-Emotional Stress Syndrome.

    Ans. Page 59.

16. Compare occu-Emotional with Emotional Stress.

    Ans. Page 59.

17. There are two basic steps to repair the damaged capillaries of a small, ordinary bruise. Name them in proper sequence.

    Ans. Pages 59-60.

CHAPTER FIVE
ARMS and HANDS

One of the most common problems we incur from the arms and hands is exhaustion. With the exception of the legs and feet, the greatest amount of physical labor performed by the body is done with the arms and hands. The arms and hands have one additional factor that is usually not encountered by the legs and feet and that is precision coordination and delicate decision control patterns. The arms and hands are the true extensions of the eyes and brain, certainly partially because of their physical adaptability for precision work.

It is interesting that man will not let physical restriction hold him down. We are all aware of cases in which people have overcome their handicaps and performed amazing feats with their feet, or mouth and head, in lieu of arms and hands. These are rare cases to be sure. For most of us, emotional stresses are transmitted to the arms and hands and thereby become our prime target. It was mentioned in the previous chapter how these chronic conditions lead to more serious breakdowns of our systems.

What are the symptoms of muscular exhaustion? The first indications may be nothing more than a feeling of heaviness of the limb and can frequently go unnoticed.

The body has its own protective system and in this instance, it produces lactic-acid (changing energy cells into accelerated waste) at the synaptic endplates. (This process is very much like carbon retarding the electrical spark of the distributor points on a car.) The lactic acid reduces neural transmission and gives us a heavy, tired muscle feeling and also increases the number of errors in our work.

In the more advanced stages, the muscle may become stiff and painful, which in turn might become arthritic.

Japanese research scientists have recently proven in laboratory tests that Shiatsu changes lactic acid into glycogens, thereby eliminating the exhaustion factor. This one fact may prove to be the key to preventing a vast number of common diseases we now suffer from.

We will cover three main issues in this section, starting with fatigue.

FATIGUE

The diagram in Figure 5-1 is similar to that in Figure 2-2 with slight modifications. Points 1 and 2 are pressed with the thumb. Point 1 is on the side of the wrist. Points 3 and 4 are pressed with the middle finger, with point 4 on the outer side of the wrist.

In the next diagram (Figure 5-2) we will examine eighteen points on the outside of the arm. Points 1 through 10 may be pressed simultaneously with the thumb and the forefinger. Place the thumb on point 1 and forefinger on point 6. Points 11 through 18 may be pressed with either the forefinger or middle finger.

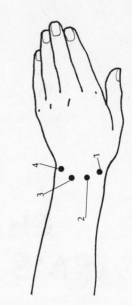

Fig. 5 - 1. Pressure points on the wrist. (Pressure: twelve pounds.)

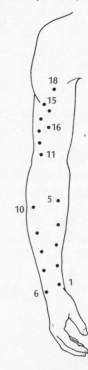

Fig. 5 - 2. Pressure points of the arm. (Pressure: twelve pounds.)

Review Figures 2-5 and 2-7. As a reminder, let me mention once more, that while the diagrams show only one side, they are applicable to both sides. In the diagram in Figure 5-3, press each point with the thumb.

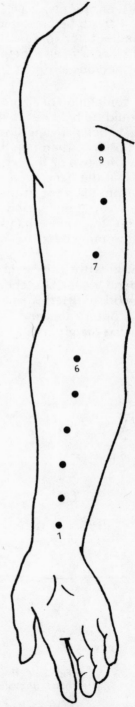

Fig. 5 - 3. Pressure points on the arm. (Pressure: ten pounds.)

All fifteen points indicated in Figure 5-4 are to be performed with the thumb of the opposite hand. These points are also helpful for relieving nervous anxiety.

Upon completion of all points, the arms should be held out to the side with the hands dangling down in a relaxed position. Then flop them up and down for two or three minutes. Be sure that the hand is completely relaxed from the wrist to the finger separately, by the tip, and stretch each with the other hand. Then reverse the procedure.

Along with this exercise, I recommend a hand stretching exercise. Extend both arms out to the side and open the hand with the palms facing the ground. Spread the fingers as far as possible while pushing the arms away from the body. This helps to relieve hand cramping of the palms and fingers.

Exercise is one of the keys in preventing tension and I will include a few exercises for the relief of tension throughout the book. I am a strong advocate of exercise used as a preventive mechanism. A well-regulated set of exercises combined with Shiatsu is extremely beneficial, even as a disease progresses into a degenerative state.

Note: In the case of a degenerative condition, exercise can only be recommended after proper diagnosis and x-ray by a competent physician.

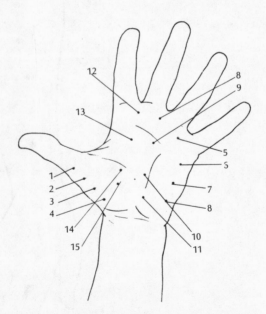

Fig. 5 - 4. Pressure points of the palm of the hand. (Pressure: twelve pounds.)

ARTHRITIS

This topic has been covered rather thoroughly under cervical and shoulder arthritis, but I would like to touch on the areas in the elbow and wrist, the back of the hand calcifying, and the fingers.

There is a simple method of testing the elbow for arthritis. Hold your arm out straight and rotate from one side to the other. If you feel pain on either side of the elbow (barring any recent bruise), it is fairly certain the pain is a result of calcium buildup.

Testing the wrist may be done the same way. Rotate the wrist first clockwise and then counterclockwise and observe any painful areas.

After locating the troubled area by rotation, the next step is to probe the area with a finger tip. Locating the arthritis on the back of the hand can also be done by probing with a finger tip. It is better to start at the wrist and follow the tendon down to the base of each finger. It is always beneficial to work around arthritis deposits in the hope that increased circulation might conceivably assimilate some of the calcium.

Another recommended exercise for arthritis of the fingers is to twist the fingers as shown in Figure 5-5.

Pressure Points for Arm and Hand Arthritis

Review the diagrams in Figures 3-16 and 3-17 and follow the directions given for them. Next, review the diagrams in Figures 4-2 and 4-4, and then the diagram in Figure 4-5.

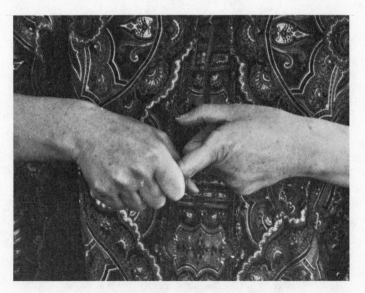

Fig. 5 - 5. Twisting the fingers for relief of arthritis.

When a deposit of calcium is found on the back of the hand, follow this procedure. A calcium deposit should feel like a little hard round object. Using the forefinger of the opposite hand, press along the *outside* of the deposit at three equidistant points from one-quarter to one-half inch apart. Next, repeat the same procedure, but on the *inside* of the deposit; then on the *top,* and last, *underneath.*

The diagram in Figure 5-6 will show you a pattern. Some of the points may follow hand contours. Press with the forefinger of the opposite hand.

Should you find calcium in the first knuckle of the forefinger (the large knuckle above the palm), place the forefinger of the opposite hand beside the knuckle and apply *eight pounds of pressure.* Move clockwise around the knuckle, applying the same pressure at twelve points.

Follow the same procedure on all four knuckles, first on the back of the hand. Then turn the hand over and repeat the treatment.

For the other finger joints, grasp the sides of the finger, between the second and third joints, and twist gently to the right, then to the left. This will stretch the muscles and ligaments.

Let me reiterate that Shiatsu will in no way interfere with any medication you may be taking for arthritis, and as previously mentioned, it may increase its effectiveness.

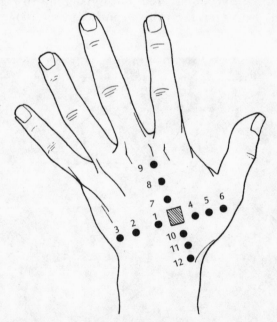

Fig. 5 - 6. Pressure points of the hand. (Pressure: twelve pounds.)

TENDONITIS

Sometimes tendonitis is called "tennis elbow." The elbow is most frequently involved in this injury, but certainly tendonitis is not limited to only that area. To explain tendonitis, the ligaments that hold the tendon in position becomes torn and inflammed because of strain.

In order to bring about some degree of relief for tendonitis, it is necessary to reduce the inflammation. To do this utilize ice applications to the inflamed area.

The next step is to locate the tendon and muscle that are in spasm. This is accomplished by first probing along the tendon and muscles running down from the irritation. (In some instances, you may find the strain running *up* the arm from the elbow.)

After locating the strained muscle and tendon, follow it up or down to its midpoint (half way along its length). Starting at the midpoint, apply pressure at six equidistant points straight up from the midpoint and six points below it. This should be done with any muscle that is tense and should be repeated three or four times.

The diagram in Figure 5-7 will give you a visual explanation of the preceding procedure.

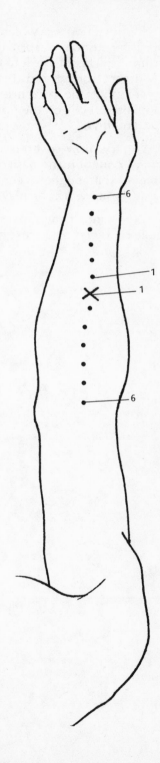

Fig. 5 - 7. Pressure points on the arm. (Pressure: twelve pounds.)

The selection of which finger should be used in applying the pressure will again be left to your own discretion. Keep in mind, however, that the pressure should be applied *directly* on the point, and not at an angle.

We have now covered a few of the most common and easily treated problems that might occur at any time at home, work, or play.

There are many, many more complex subjects to discuss but they require a deeper and broader comprehension of the theories of Shiatsu than may be presented in this book. Even in this limited form, however, it is my objective to bring you immediate relief in certain areas that you may, with some practice, perform to treat yourself.

"When pain in the arms
Feel like steel bands
It does no harm
To work the hands"

QUESTIONS
CHAPTER V

1. The precision coordination and delicate decision control patterns of the arms and hands make us think of them as true extensions of what?

   Ans. Page 63.

2. What is usually the first sympton of muscular exhaustion?

   Ans. Page 63.

3. What does the nervous system produce to protect itself?

   Ans. Page 63.

4. What, in your opinion, would be the reason for the difference in the amounts of pressure indicated for use on pressure points Figures: 5-1 and 5-2 (Pages 64 & 65)?

   Ans. Tissue, Tone and Texture.

5. Demonstrate the hand stretching exercise. Indicate exactly how it is performed.

   Ans. Page 66.

6. How do you test the elbow for arthritis?

   Ans. Page 67.

7. When arthritis is located on the back of the hand, what is the recommended procedure of treatment?

   Ans. Page 67.

8. "Tendonitis" commonly referred to as "Tennis Elbow" is not just limited to the elbow area. Which procedure is recommended for locating and treating Tendonitis?

   Ans. Page 69.

CHAPTER SIX
STOMACH and LOWER BACK

Shiatsu does work. Follow the directions given here and it will work for you.

The area of the spine that causes more trouble than any other is the lumbar or lower region. We are told by anthropologists and physiologists that because man stands erect, the lumbar region receives the weight of the upper torso, thus making it the center of strain.

Regardless of the why, statistics agree that this is the most critical area of the spine. A contributing cause could be chronic neglect because of a greater pain threshold in this part of the spine; another contributing cause is the overdevelopment of the gluteal (hip) muscles and the underdevelopment of other muscle groups that act as counterbalances.

The following illustration (Figure 6-1) shows groups of muscles that create strains and counterstrains. The glutei are the strongest muscle group in the body. Figure 6-1 indicates the location of these groups.

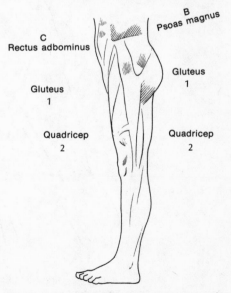

Fig. 6 - 1. The gluteus and quadvicep muscles.

The two largest and strongest groups are the glutei and quadriceps. These are numbered according to their size and strength (gluteal = 1. quadriceps = 2.)

Groups 1 and 2 are in opposition to the latissimus dorsi (A), psoas magnus (B), and rectus abdominus (C) muscles.

Figure 6-2 shows a man lifting a heavy weight.

The figure indicates the muscle groups and the arrows show the direction they pull.

Fig. 6 - 2. Direction of muscle pull when lifting a heavy object.

The latissimus dorsi (Figure 6-3) and rectus abdominus muscles contract in an upward movement. The glutei and quadriceps pull or contract in a downward motion, which leaves the lower back vulnerable to dislocation. The psoas magnus muscles, which are an inverted "V" shape, run from the lower back to the front of the hip socket where they wrap around and come slightly behind the joint. Figures 6-4 and 6-5 help explain the function of these muscles.

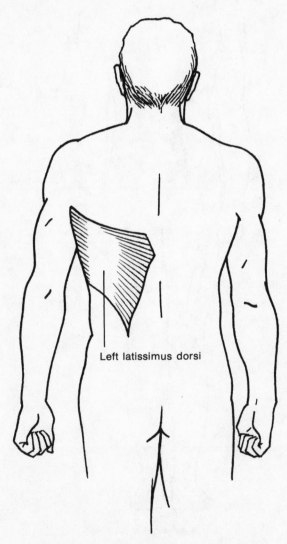

Left latissimus dorsi

Fig. 6 - 3. The left latissimus dorsi (lower back) muscles.

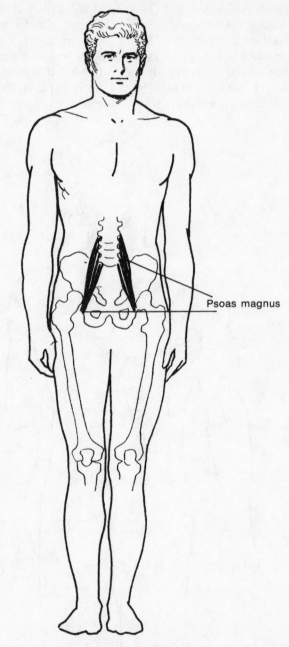

Psoas magnus

Fig. 6 - 4. The psoas magnus muscles.

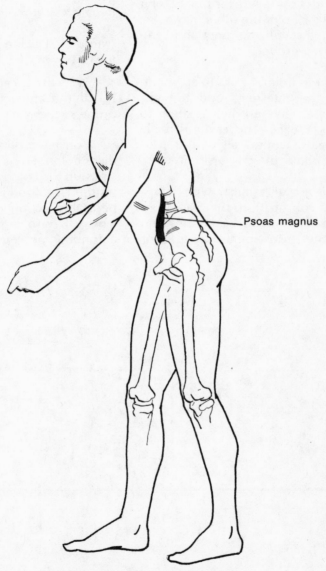

Psoas magnus

Fig. 6 - 5. The psoas magnus muscles.

The psoas muscles act as stabilizers for the lower spine.

With a tridirectional strain on the first, second, third, and fourth lumbar vertebrae, it is easy to understand how overexertion of one muscle group or the other may overcome the stabilizing function of the other two groups.

At this point, I want to elaborate about the intestines and the abdominal cavity and their relation to the lower back. This cavity is really the seat of almost all of our problems, either directly or indirectly.

We are all familiar with symptoms of constipation; they vary from abdominal pains to back pains and headaches. Most of us pay little or no attention to these symptoms and simply take a laxative and forget it. This can be an easy remedy, but unfortunately in some cases, it is merely masking a more serious condition, giving only temporary relief. Regardless of the cause, what I wish to stress here is the effect an overloaded colon may have on the lower back.

We will concern ourselves chiefly with the large intestine and its four prime sections (Figure 6-6).

You will notice that the ascending colon (1) is where the food starts up the colon from the small intestine. The food is moved along by peristaltic action or counteraction, which in turn is controlled by the autonomic nervous system.

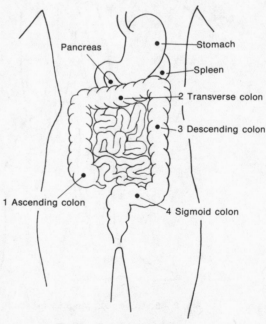

Pancreas

Stomach

Spleen

2 Transverse colon

3 Descending colon

1 Ascending colon

4 Sigmoid colon

Fig. 6 - 6. Large intestine.

The transverse colon section (2) is of great importance and probably is the greatest trouble spot. The descending colon (3) does not cause as much trouble, but is prone to telescoping, which may also impair elimination. The sigmoid colon (4) or (pocket) is a natural trouble spot because of its storage capacity and retention ability.

Now, should any of these areas tend to become constricted with either gas pockets or feces and start to balloon and press against the abdominal nerve plexus or even against vertebrae, a pain will develop along the spine. Therefore, it is essential when checking the back to also press lightly along the colon, starting at point 1 and following around to point 4, with about two inches between each point.

The upper corners of the colon are located about midpoint between the breastbone and the outside edge of the ribcage of the lowest rib. From the midpoint of the rib, on the right side, move down in a straight line about three-fourths the way down the abdomen for a starting point. Then, come up using the four-finger technique, as shown in Figure 6-7.

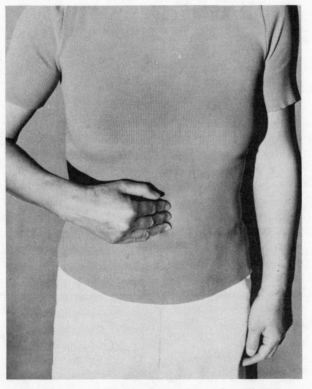

Fig. 6 - 7. Application of the four-finger technique to the colon area.

After following the colon up to the rib, follow the transverse colon straight across to the midpoint of the left rib and then straight down, almost to the hip bone.

It would be fitting at this point to show the sections of the vertebral column. We have already discussed the cervical or neck vertebrae. The second segment is the thoracic or dorsal vertebrae, composed of twelve vertebrae. The third section is the lumbar vertebrae consisting of only five vertebrae, but they are very critical. We will examine these later in this chapter.

The bottom of the ladder consists of five more vertebrae that fuse together shortly after birth and, barring an accident, give little trouble until middle age when calcium deposits sometimes form along the nerves. Upon occasion, a spinal dislocation in the lumbar region may produce a muscular strain in the sacral vertebrae and produce a pain that is carried down the leg.

We have twenty-six vertebrae in the spine, which are divided into four major segments, with a tail of five small bones called the coccyx (Figure 6-8).

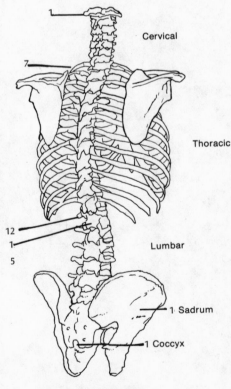

Fig. 6 - 8. Vertebrae.

As mentioned before, we will concern ourselves in this chapter with the lumbar and sacral segments primarily, but will also include the lower half of the thoracic area because of its relationship to the large and small intestines, plus the impact that the sympathetic and parasympathetic systems along the spine have on the organs of the body.

In Chapter 1 the sympathetic and parasympathetic nervous systems were mentioned and their functions explained. If you review that information you will understand the function of these systems. Figure 6-9 illustrates the interrelationship of the skeletal, myological (muscular), neural (nerves) systems to the internal organs.

Before we study Figure 6-9, note chart I. This chart shows various body parts (i.e., legs, bladder, etc.) and which systems they involve. All parts shown, with the exception of the skeletal (related), are controlled by the sympathetic and parasympathetic nervous systems. Anything that is skeletal (related) must be innervated by controlled thought.

Chart I

	Myological	Netural	Internal Organic	Skeletal
Stomach	x	x	x	
Liver bile		x	x	
Pancreas		x	x	
Intestines	x	x	x	
Leg muscles	x	x		x
Feet	x	x		x
Hip Muscle	x	x		x
Rectum	x	x	x	
Bladder	x	x	x	
Bowels	x	x	x	
Kidney	x	x	x	
Spleen		x	x	

In Figure 6-9 the spinal vertebrae are shown with a breakdown indicating their relation to different organs and muscles. It also shows which nerves of the spine exert an influence and which is affected.

For example, the pancreas is related to the eighth spinal nerve (8-T). The ninth, tenth, and eleventh thoracic vertebrae are also connected, as well as a distant cousin, to the second sacral.

These are by no means the only organs that are part of the lower spinal nerves, but are the ones that are involved in lower back problems.

For a hypothetical case, let us assume you have had a dull, lower backache. There are occasional gurglings in the lower or small intestine and infrequent little shooting pains. It is reasonable to assume that you are suffering from an intestinal upset.

Here is where theory differs. Acupuncture, acupressure (Shiatsu), osteopathy, and chiropractic follow the theory that spinal or vertebral pressure on the spinal nerve ends does have a reflex action on the organs connected to that nerve. With this thought in mind, let us return to the intestinal problem you have.

The intestines' nerve ends are seated in the 12th-T, 1st-T, 1st'L, 2nd'L, and 2nd S (Figure 6-9); and these would become the first areas to which you would apply the treatment. Apply pressure to both sides of the spine, as shown in Figure 4-19.

This is where the similarity between osteopathy and chiropractic ends.

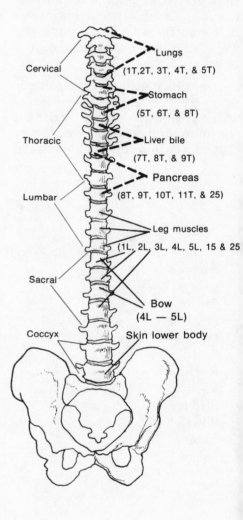

Fig. 6 - 9. The spinal vertebrae.

We now proceed to the ancient Chinese energy flows, as indicated in Figures 6-10 and 6-11. Follow the points in numerical order in the diagrams. The points along the little finger may be reached with the forefinger of the opposite hand, braced from the inside with a gentle pressure from the thumb.

Fig. 6 - 11. Energy flow in face and neck. (Pressure: eight pounds.)

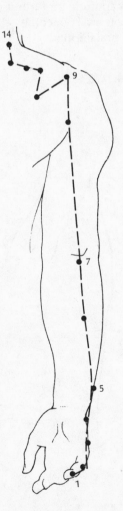

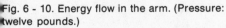

Fig. 6 - 10. Energy flow in the arm. (Pressure: twelve pounds.)

After completing the preceding points, it is advisable to use the flats of the four fingers on the points shown in Figure 6-12, which cover the lower intestine. Follow the points numerically.

We have now covered both the large and small intestines. What about the other organs and leg muscles?

Figure 6-9 shows the connecting nerves for the other primary organs, and the same procedure may be followed with each (with the exception of the reflex energy points, which must be taught in an academic surrounding). I did indicate the points, but the specific location, direction, and pressure needed to achieve proper results require months of instruction of supervision. If you possess the desire to proceed beyond this point, and have an aptitude for further study, perhaps you will become a prosional Shiatsu practitioner.

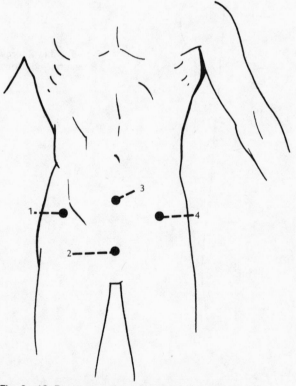

Fig. 6 - 12. Pressure points on lower intestine. (Pressure: eight pounds.)

One more point to discuss at this time regarding the back, and those are the points used for the latissimus dorsi muscles and the oblique muscles of the back, as show in the diagram in Figure 6-13.

Start with point 1 and follow through sequence to point 7. Then repeat the procedure on the opposite side.

For points 1 through 4 use the knuckles (as shown in Figure 4-19). For points 5 through 7, use the thumb.

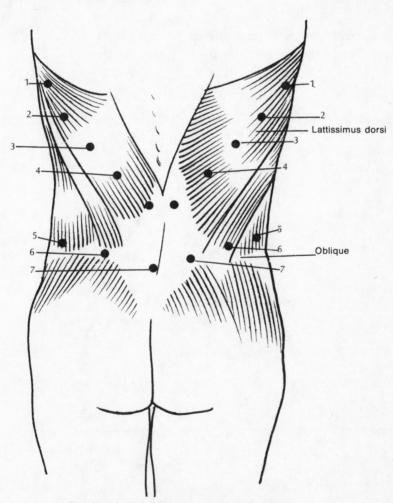

Fig. 6 - 13. The latissimus dorsi and oblique muscles of the lower back. (Pressure: twelve pounds.)

We now have a complete series of points for the lower back and vicera (abdomen). The points shown in this book, for the most part, are the fundamentals and are more easily assimilated. As mentioned previously, the deeper studies of acupressure must be taught in an academic environment.

You will notice a relationship between this chapter and the next on hips, legs, and feet. This is applicable for all myoskeletal (muscular-skeletal) parts of the body. At certain points, they overlap.

I purposely combined the stomach and lower back because of the influence one has on the other. I believe you are now prepared to proceed to the next chapter.

"A pain
In the back
May be the
Gastro-track"

QUESTIONS
CHAPTER VI

1. Anthropologists and physiologists report that because man stands erect, a certain condition results. What is this condition?
Ans. Page 73.

2. What is the name of the strongest group of muscles in the lower torso?
Ans. Page 73.

3. A "pain in the back" may relate to the intestinal tract. How?
Ans. Page 78.

4. How many spinal vertebrae are there?
Ans. Page 80.

5. Name the five segments or divisions of the spine.
Ans. Page 80.

6. What is significant about the groupings noted on the chart #I, Page 81?
Ans. Review Page 81 Chart.

7. Which spinal nerve ends are connected tm the pancreas?
Ans. Page 82.

8. Review Figure 6-9, Page 82 and determine which spinal nerves are connected to the stomach. Name them.
Ans. Page 82 - Figure 6-9.

9. There is one nerve that is related to the stomach, liver and pancreas. Name it.
Ans. Page 82 - Figure 6-9.

10. Do the legs and bowels have a common nerve?
Ans. Figure 6-9 - Page 82.

11. Is there a common nerve between the pancreas and the intestines?
Ans. Page 82.

12. Is there a nerve-end shared by the lungs and stomach?

    Ans. Figure 6-9 - Page 82.

13. Acupuncture, acupressure (Shiatsu), Osteopathy and Chiropractic have a theory in common. What is it?

    Ans. Page 82.

CHAPTER SEVEN
HIPS, LEGS, and FEET

With the average person, there is no other part of the body receiving the punishment the hips, legs, and feet do. This part of the anatomy takes the day-in and day-out strain and is therefore most obvious to us.

Modern man exercises less and carries more body weight than did his ancestors. In the preceding chapter, I mentioned the gluteal muscles of the hip and the enormous strength they have, as well as the quadricep muscles.

It is the quadricep muscles I would like to analyze at this point. You will then understand the relationship between the primary leg-foot, and nerves and muscles to locomotion.

Quadriceps
This group of muscles is the key to the strength and endurance of the legs. In running, these are the muscles that determine how far and how fast you will go.

Note: No single group of muscles can operate autonomously without the help of other groups. Another important point to remember is that *all of these groups of muscles are linked through nerve trunks, which pass through several groups.*

Figure 7-1 shows the four quadricep muscles:

1. Rectus femoris—covers the front of the thigh
2. Vastus externus—the fleshy muscle on the outside of the thigh
3. Vastus medialis—lies slightly to the inside of the rectus femoris muscle
4. Vastus internus—actually two sections, with the upper por-

tion lying under the rectus femoris and the lower portion extending to the inside of the knee.

The quadriceps are the extensors that push the legs down and are therefore, the first to tire when running. In opposition to these, we have the crural bicep along the back of the thigh, which tires less easily and is usually not a factor in fatigue.

The stabilizing of these two groups is handled by the adductor muscles. There are three muscles in this group, as illustrated in Figure 7-2.

1. Adductor magnus—runs from the pubis down the back of the thigh to the knee
2. Adductor longus—runs from the outer edge of the ischium, angling in to a point midway down the side of the femur
3. Adductor brevis—runs from the pubis to a point about four inches down the front of the femur

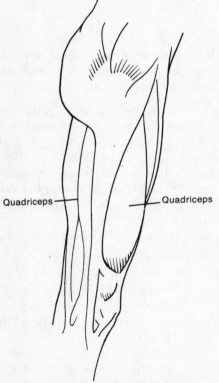

Fig. 7 - 1. The quadricep muscles.

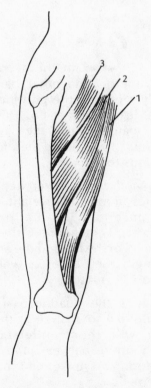

Fig. 7 - 2. The adductors for muscles.

The adductor muscles are generally the second most frequent area that produces fatigue. As previously mentioned, these are the guide and balance muscles, quite frequently strained in bodily contact sports.

The sartorius muscle is related to both the thigh and the calf muscles. This muscle runs from the illium and attaches to a tendon immediately below and inside the knee. The primary function of the sartorius is to rotate the thigh and also help stabilize the thigh and calf muscles.

Moving down to the calf, we find the superficial muscle the gas-trocnemius. The gastrocnemius attaches to the Achilles tendon. This muscle pulls the Achilles tendon and this, in turn, activates the plantar muscle of the foot for walking and running.

The muscles mentioned above are supplied by the medial popliteal nerve running down the backside of the tibia bone.

The innervation of the feet is also derived from the lower posterior end of the popliteal nerve, at this point called the posterior tibial nerve. At the ankle, it divides into internal and external plantar nerves.

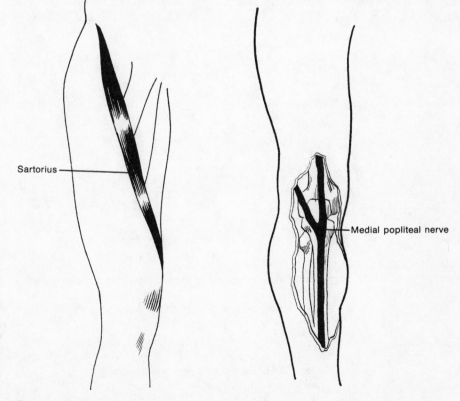

Sartorius

Medial popliteal nerve

Fig. 7 - 3. The sartorius muscle.

Fig. 7 - 4. The medial popliteal nerve.

As you can see, the body has a complete transmission system from the spine to the toes carried in one main trunk, the great sciatic nerve and its branches. This gives a simplified explanation. Let me point out that *any disruption along the greater sciatic nerve may well have a detrimental effect on the branches and the muscles serviced by them.*

We have shown the innervation down the leg by efferent (locomotor) nerves, but what is happening on the return by the afferent (sensory) nerves. Are they merely standing by? By no means. They are recording every muscular strain, circulatory block, temperature change, metabolic change, and hundreds of other bodily reponses. They, in turn, notify the central dispatcher (the cerebral cortex which, in turn, innervates the proper central nerve, organ, or muscle, individually, collectively or in combination).

A condition reflex pain is quite common to most of us. It is important to thoroughly understand how these come about. For example, a person has a job standing at a machine, in a bent position, performing a complex task day after day. In most jobs of this type, there is a limitation of movement and certain muscles tend to contract and shorten. Ligaments also tighten and restrict limb articulation. Most of this

Fig. 7 - 5. Location of stiffness in the sacroiliac area.

could be avoided with proper exercise, but unfortunately, most people fail to do this and are forced to seek other means of relief.

The preceding example refers to a specific occupational strain, but many of us suffer from the same condition as a result of a poor postural stance. I would venture to say from years of observation that 70 percent of the people in the United States stand on one leg and then the other. In a great number of these cases, this practice leads to a permanent muscle or bone deformity. Structurally, we are not built to stand on one foot, no more than a building will stand without damage if half of the foundation starts sinking.

Now you understand the problem, so let's get on with the solutions. Shiatsu does have the answer: it is positive action to release the atrophied muscle and tightened ligaments. Keep in mind the overlap of the lower back and hip areas mentioned in the previous chapter.

The first condition we will concern ourselves with now is the very common sacroiliac pain. This is usually a myloskeletal condition, but as in most problems of this type, Shiatsu pressure will release the spasm.

Figure 7-5 shows the location of stiffness and pain in the sacroiliac; Figure 7-6 shows the posterior view.

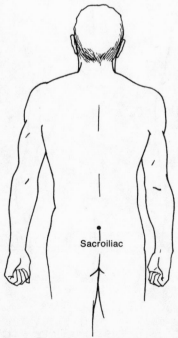

Sacroiliac

Fig. 7 - 6. Posterior view showing location of sacroiliac.

Shiatsu Points for Sacroiliac

The simplest way to reach the points shown in Figure 7-7, points 1, 2, 3, 4, 5, and 6, is with the middle knuckle of the forefinger (see Figure 2-13).

The hand is made into a fist with the knuckles facing up and the fingers down (as demonstrated in Figure 2-14).

The hand is placed under the hip while sitting on a chair (see Figure 7-8). The important thing is to place the forefinger knuckle in the hip dimple. (Note dimple point.)

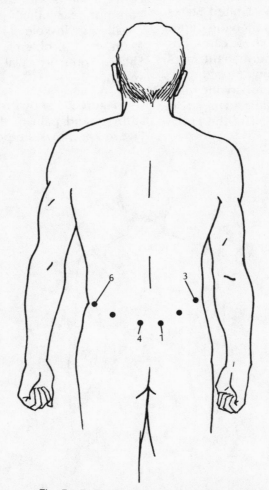

Fig. 7 - 7. Pressure points for the sacroiliac.
(Pressure: twelve pounds.)

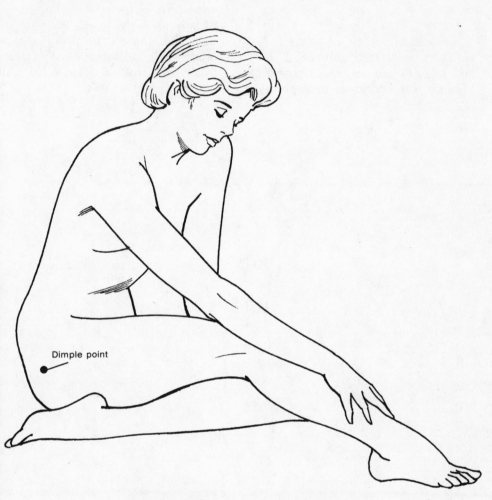

Fig. 7 - 8. Dimple point in the hip. (Pressure: fifteen pounds.)

The back of the thighs is another difficult area to reach (Figure 7-9) and is best handled using the knuckles of the closed fist. This is the same procedure used in Figure 7-7.

Place knuckles of closed fist along the indicated points 1, 2, 3, 4, and apply fifteen pounds of pressure; hold for ten seconds at each point.

The pressure points shown in Figure 7-9 are along the posterior (back) side of the sciatic nerve. It is therefore advisable to include these points whenever sciatic problems arise. While the sciatic nerve is not usually directly involved with the sacroiliac, there is tension that does relate to the posterior muscles of the thigh, and probably causes irritation along the nerve.

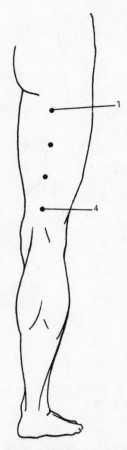

Fig. 7 - 9. Pressure points on the back of the thigh. (Pressure: fifteen pounds.)

The diagram in Figure 7-10 is of the lateral or side muscles of the thigh and relate through the nerve to the sacroiliac.

When a difficult point to locate is evident, as is this, utilize a "shotgun" technique. Apply fifteen pounds of pressure to points 1 through 10, and hold for ten seconds t each point. Use middle knuckle of ie forefinger (as shown in Figure 2-3)

Sciatic nerve pain is the most annoying and common of all back and leg problems. In 90 percent of the cases I have observed, the cause is in the lumbar and sacral vertebrae of the lower spine, produced either by vertebral compression or arthritis.

By referring to Figure 6-9, you will better understand how the pain is transmitted down the legs and also which vertebrae may be involved.

The problem is not quite as simple to correct as it might sound. There are various contributing factors: strain from the neck, shoulders, or lower limb of the opposite side. These factors are structural and may sometimes be evaluated by standing in front of a mirror and observing the following:

1. One shoulder lower than the other
2. Head tilting to the right or left
3. Abdominal twist across naval
* 4. Distintention of either right or left side of lower abdomen
5. Pelvis (hips) hiked-up on one side or the other
6. In natural stance, one foot pointing either in or out more than the other

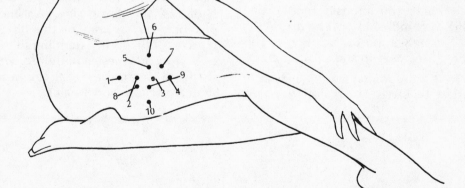

Fig. 7 - 10. The lateral muscles of the thigh. (Pressure: twelve pounds.)

* This is only item not requiring a mirror. You may just look down at your feet.

I would say at this point, the reader has a concept of what his body is about and should be able to observe himself more objectively. Your first question may be, What possible effect will these observations have on the sciatic nerve? Your question deserves an answer, so let me elaborate each point.

The shoulder drop (1) most frequently indicates a weakness in the pectoral or trapezius muscles but a spasm across the latissimus muscle from the lumbar area will result in the same shoulder drop. This may be easily supported by placing the lower knuckles (Figure 2-17) halfway down the spine and about two inches out from the spine, either on the right or left side. Tension will be noted, as well as mild to acute pain.

In most instances, the head tilt (2) is a result of shortened muscles in the neck or shoulder area, but in certain cases, it may indicate a vertebral dislocation. Perhaps, 50 percent of these dislocations have a traumatic effect on the lumbar vertebrae and intensify the narrowing or compression of the disc in the 1 through 3 lumbar vertebrae. This produces pain in the sciatic nerve.

An abdominal twist (3) may arise from the psoas (Figure 6-4), or rectus abdominus muscles (Figure 6-1), either of which may create a strain on the lumbar vertebrae. Another possibility is a skeletal transverse strain from one shoulder to the opposite hip, also affecting the lumbar vertebrae.

The distention of lower abdomen (4) is more frequently caused by the intestines, but on occasion, may be a result of a shortening of the oblique muscles that run down from the ribs to the illium. This usually occurs in the muscles on the opposite side from the distention.

The most common cause of a hiked pelvis (5) is the slipping or disc deterioration of the fourth or fifth lumbar vertebra. The other two causes are: the psoas muscle in spasm on one side; and the latissimus and oblique muscles both in spasm on the side that is hiked-up.

The outward position of the foot (6) indicates a shortening of a lower leg muscle or a ligmental velarration of either the annular ligament of the ankle, the flexor longus pollicus pedis of the lower leg. Another possibility is a spasm of the flexor muscles of the foot, extending to the toes. Any of these conditions will throw a strain up the leg and simulate sciatic nerve pains.

The following pressure points should be used for sciatic related problems. Figure 7-11 shows points related to the shoulder drop (1). (The points in this diagram appear larger because the entire hand is being used.)

The conditions described in items 2, 3, 4, and 5 are covered in Figure 7-12 and Figures 7-8, 7-9, and 7-10.

For a turned foot, see Figure 7-14. On points 1 through 6, apply fifteen pounds of pressure, and hold for 15 seconds at each point.

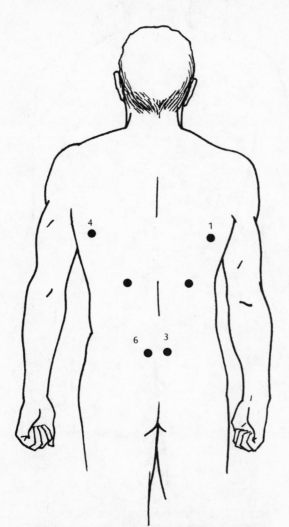

Fig. 7 - 11. Pressure points on back used for sciatic related problems. (Pressure: fifteen pounds.)

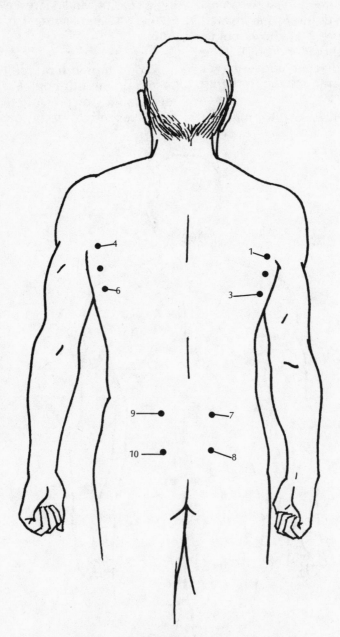

Fig. 7 - 12. Pressure points on the back.
(Pressure: fifteen pounds.)

There are ten points shown in the diagram in Figure 7-12. Points 1 through 6 are reached by using the middle finger of the hand opposite that side and reaching across the chest. Points 7 through 10 are pressed with the fingers placed on the hips and the thumbs on the points, as shown in Figure 7-13.

The dimple point indicated in the diagram in Figure 7-8 is another key sciatic nerve entry and should be worked at this time in the same way as those points shown in the diagram in Figure 7-8.

The backs of the thighs, another related area, should be followed as shown in the diagram in Figure 7-9. Then, after the backs of the thighs, it is advisable to use the "shotgun" technique for the lateral exterior side of the thigh, as shown in Figure 7-10.

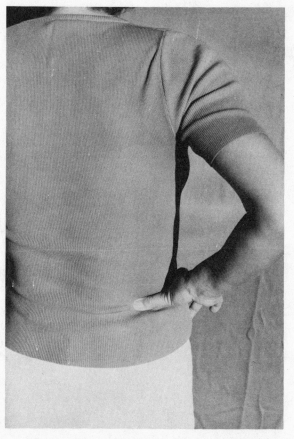

Fig. 7 - 13. Applying pressure to back with thumbs.

The illustrations in Figures 7-14 and 7-15 show the two foot extremes in a turned foot condition (6).

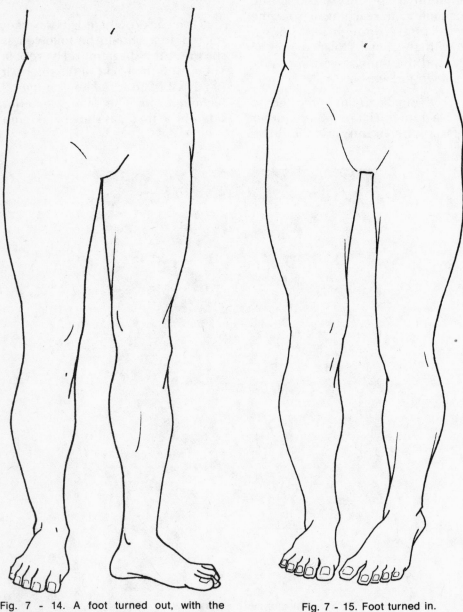

Fig. 7 - 14. A foot turned out, with the predominant twist running from the knee down.

Fig. 7 - 15. Foot turned in.

Note the key pressure points for relieving the turned-out foot indicated in Figure 7-16. Points 1 through 7 are best handled with the middle knuckle of the forefinger, as shown in Figure 7-17. Points 8 through 10 may best be handled with the palm side of the middle finger, Figure 2-15.

Fig. 7 - 16. Pressure points on leg. (Pressure: fifteen pounds.)

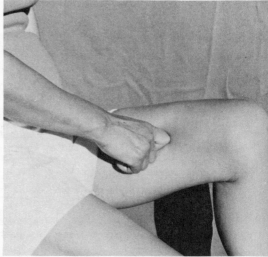

Fig. 7 - 17. Applying pressure with middle knuckle of the forefinger.

Now look at Figure 7-18. Points 1 through 6 are easily accessible with the thumb of the hand opposite the leg in use. The points shown for use for sciatic nerve problems are also usable for any strain, of any nature, in the same area.

By using all these techniques we can cover ground for all problems, large and small. In this manner, we utilize one large common complaint, rather than several minor ones. Visually, the reader may adapt to the lesser complaints.

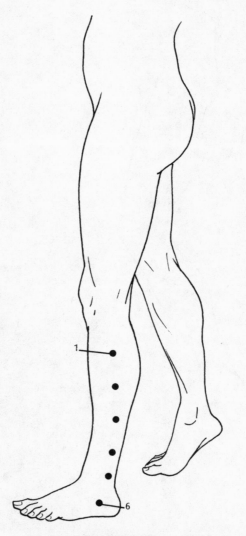

Fig. 7 - 18. Pressure points on outside of calf. (Pressure: fifteen pounds.)

The Feet

No part of our anatomy takes more daily abuse than do the feet. We put tremendous weight on them, stomp them, chill them, bind them in leather corsets, and restrict circulation with elastic. It is truly amazing that we do not have more trouble with our feet. I will not go into a long dissertation on the feet but I will give you a few key points that not only will give relief to the feet, but also, the legs.

Start with the diagram in Figure 7-19. For points 1 through 20, start between the last joint of the big toe and the toe next to it.

The next area is between the next two toes, moving horizontally toward the little toe. Follow this to point 4 on the outside of the little toe.

The second row of points are immediately below the first, about one inch. The third row are one inch below the second, etc. Point 20 should be just below the calloused part of the heel.

All of these points are best reached by using the forefinger, placed on the floor beneath the foot. For those unable to reach over that far, a small marble or steel ball may be used.

The pressures are no longer indicated because I do feel you are able to control this by now.

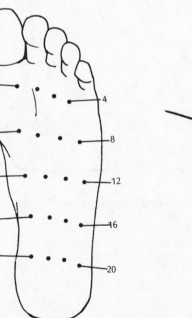

Fig. 7 - 19. Pressure points on the bottom of the foot. (Pressure: twelve pounds.)

Fig. 7 - 20. Pressure points on the foot. (Pressure: twelve pounds.)

The diagram in Figure 7-20 shows the outside of the left foot with eight pressure points. Points 1 through 6 are best handled with the middle finger on the outside points and the resistive pressure from the thumb on the inside, and points 7 and 8 with either middle finger or the middle knuckle of the forefinger.

The diagram in Figure 7-21 shows the inside of the left foot.

"When things aren't going so neat . . . Remember . . . The legs and the feet"

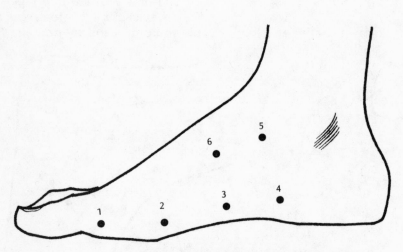

Fig. 7 - 21. The pressure points on the feet. (Pressure: ten pounds.)

QUESTIONS
CHAPTER VII

1. Two factors of modern man, relative to his ancestors, have a definite effect on his legs. Name them.
   Ans. Page 89.

2. What are the four muscles consituting the Quadricep group?
   Ans. Page 89.

3. What purpose is accomplished by the Adductor muscles? Name them.
   Ans. Page 90.

4. What is the function of the Sartorius muscle?
   Ans. Page 91.

5. The Gastrocnemius muscle activates the Plantar muscle of the foot for walking and running and attaches to which Tendon?
   Ans. Page 91.

6. How are the feet effected by the Popliteal nerve?
   Ans. Page 91.

7. Another name for the locomotor nerves and their function are covered in this chapter, what are they?
   Ans. Page 92.

8. Another name for the sensory nerves and their function are covered in this chapter, what are they?
   Ans. Page 92.

9. Where is the Scro-Illiac located?
   Ans. Page 93 - Figure 7-6.

10. Is the Sciatic Nerve ever involved with the Sacro-Illiac?
    Ans. Page 96.

11. There are six observations which may be made to note possible Sciatic Nerve pressure. Name them.

    Ans. Page 97.

12. What does the "shoulder drop" most frequently indicate?

    Ans. Page 98.

13. What muscles are involved in the "abdominal twist"?

    Ans. Page 98.

14. Distention of the lower abdomen is more frequently caused by the intestines. Name another cause mentioned in this chapter.

    Ans. Page 98.

CHAPTER EIGHT
UPPER BACK

Problems of the upper back are, as a rule, connected to other conditions of the lower back, shoulders, or neck. In some cases they are the result of a transverse strain from one shoulder to the opposite hip (See Item 3, Chapter Seven, p. 97.

Imagine that the thoracic (chest) area is like a box made of pliable plastic. Now, should you pull one corner, what happens? You no longer have a rectangular box, but one with a more trapezoidal shape. With a pliable plastic box, there is no damage, but with pliable muscles, organs, and tissue, it becomes a totally different situation.

Let us, for example, explore the skeletal strains that might occur. A subject is standing on a ladder painting and the ladder slips out from under him. The first reaction is to grab for support, so he latches on to a beam with one hand, and the brush and bucket with the other. The hand with the bucket and brush goes down, as the other grasps the beam and goes up. This will cause a transverse or trapezoidal strain on the skeleton, with a slight dislocation of one or more of the midpoint vertebrae, as indicated in Figure 8-1.

The points of stress will vary according to the forward or backward thrust of the body, and also depend on whether or not the body torque is to the right or left. Another factor is muscle development.

In some individuals, the upper back and shoulders are more developed than the lower back muscles, in which case, the stress will occur at the lower points. The reverse holds true of overdevelopment of the lower muscles.

Fig. 8 - 1. A transverse or trapizuidal strain.

Many people suffer strained spinal ligaments during childhood, and in many cases these weakened areas become chronic, reactionary points to stress and strain. With the injured tissue in the area, it is quite simple to pull the vertebrae out of place slightly.

The important thing is for you to learn to read your own body. The best way to do this is to observe when, where, and how frequently the same area is subject to pain and stiffness.

Note: Pain and stiffness refers here to everyday nuisance pain and stiffness. *Anything acute requires immediate, competent medical help.*

Arthritis in these vertebral areas needs special notation. The factor of prolonged minor irritation will undoubtedly develop into arthritis in between the vertebrae. As we approach middle age, the condition deteriorates more rapidly.

Another contributing factor to upper back problems is disc deterioration or herniation. In about 90 percent of the cases, this condition is produced by chronic physical or emotional tension. Two prime examples of this are typists and concert pianists.

There are, naturally, other occupations that produce the same reaction, but these are two that all of us can relate to. The main purpose in selecting these two is that they involve physical and emotional tensions. Both demand a high degree of concentration and perfection. I will use myself as an example. I am an

above average typist for speed, but not for accuracy. Therefore, I would not enter the competitive labor market as a typist, thereby lowering the emotional tension factor.

This would not guarantee no emotional tension, but would reduce the possibility greatly.

I assume you have already formulated a physical tension thought, but I would like to suggest one that most people are unaware of. Your muscular and skeletal type is always an important factor, and without realizing it, it usually determines the type of sports or work you enjoy. Interestingly enough, there are a great many sports and occupations people follow, not out of physical ability, but as a result of admiration for another person or for the money. This person faces either emotional or physical disaster.

Should this be physical, let us see what might happen. Size and weight are important prerequisites. Let us again use the example of typing for the description.

Women are physically better suited for typing, because of their smaller and lighter bones in the arm (and in most cases), more delicate muscular development. Why is it that the more delicate physique is preferable for typing?

In most cases, the lighter frame is naturally faster and usually has better dexterity; another factor is the position of the typist. The arms are holding the hands up to the keyboard. Therefore, a person with large heavy hands and forearm will have that much greater a strain on the deltoid muscles of the shoulders. This same strain is carried to the rhomboidei between the shoulders and along the spine. It also affects the trapezius running up to the neck. To a lesser degree, the latissimus dorsi is involved, too. This is just one type of occupational stress that might be avoided if analyzed in time.

In this chapter, I am going to depart slightly from the format I have followed in the earlier chapters. In the beginning, I wished

to associate specific problems with a particular group of Shiatsu pressure points. I assume, by this time, you are aware of this fact and have begun adapting your own aches and pains to the points used for their relief, as thus far studied.

Therefore, this chapter will show the key points of the upper back, and you are now ready to take a completion test of your capabilities

Six pressure points are indicated in this diagram (Figure 8-2), three on each side of the spine. You will not

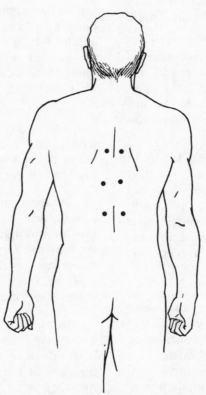

Fig. 8 - 2. Pressure points on the spine.

the points are elongated in this diagram to indicate the use of the fist knuckles, as shown in Figure 4-19.

I wish to stress that you use the proper chair to press the back against: flat, not rounded. The thickness of the upholstery does not matter, as long as it is firm. I have noted that car seats are ideal and on long drives to alleviate fatigue, use the points shown in the diagram in Figure 7-9. Many times I have started driving with a pain in the upper back, and by the time I reached my destination, it is gone. However, let me make it clear that I am recom- mending this for the passengers only, *not* the driver. The driver will have to go sit in the car after the trip to re- lieve his back. I don't think one-arm driving is either legal, without a special license, or safe.

The diagram in Figure 8-3 shows seven points that were shown in Figures 4-7 and 4-18. The difference between Figure 4-18 and 8-3 is the sequence of the points that are utilized. Remember, in this case, pressure is being used to relieve the upper back discomfort, *not* the neck and shoulders.

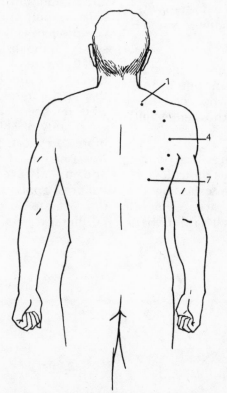

Fig. 8 - 3. Pressure points of the back. (Pressure: twelve pounds.)

All seven points are easily reached with the middle or forefinger of the hand opposite the side that is being worked on. You may refer to Figures 2-5, 2-6, and 2-7. Portions of these seven points may be used at times with other points shown in this chapter.

You have by now acquired a feeling of your own body and where your stress areas are. I therefore know that you will not remain totally bound by the guidelines I have outlined thus far. I also encourage experimentation after a degree of ability has been attained.

"It is not the man who starts the path that makes the highway, but the many who follow."

Thus, it is with knowledge that you may continue. I am one of the followers, and you who read this book and further its knowledge will help complete the highway.

Some of these pressure points shown will be quite difficult for some people to reach, especially in the area of the upper back. A simple solution is to use a small hard rubber ball (about the size of a tennis ball) and lean back against a chair. This may also be done on the floor.

We have now covered the points of the upper back, but always remember all of the groups are interrelated and reflect or transfer pain from one area to the other.

As previously mentioned, a headache may originate in the arm, shoulder, or abdomen, aside from the more obvious areas of the head and neck.

I have long felt the necessity for giving a logical explanation of the application and results achieved by Shiatsu, but none have yet been comprehensively completed. In my studies at the institute in Japan, I was greatly aware of this total absence of theory. My reason for mentioning this at this time is to assure those who are becoming more serious in your study of Shiatsu that there are more complicated aspects of Shiatsu. It is a new field outside the Orient, and as different attitudes and cultures apply this knowledge, it does lead to new vistas and expanded therapy.

QUESTIONS
CHAPTER VIII

1. Are upper back problems usually related to other causes?
   Ans. Page 109.

2. What physical actions of the body cause the spinal points of stress to change in the examples mentioned in this chapter?
   Ans. Page 109.

3. Name three observations you can make to learn to read your own body.
   Ans. Page 111.

4. Name the major contributing factor of "disc herniation".
   Ans. Page 111.

5. Is there a physical compatability for certain jobs?
   Ans. Page 111.

6. A person with large heavy hands and forearms are best suited for an occupation as a typist. True or False.
   Ans. Page 111.

7. Occupational stress can be greatly relieved and many times avoided totally by doing what?
   Ans. Page 111.

8. Review Figure 82 (Page 112) of the upper back area, and describe the best kind of seat to use for this exercise.
   Ans. Page 112.

9. In reference to the diagrams in this chapter, what was suggested as a substitute for the hand, to reach the points sometimes difficult to reach in the middle of the back?
   Ans. Page 114.

10. What is the name of the study of "energy points", to be covered in the next series of books?
    Ans. Page 114.

CHAPTER NINE
BREATHING

*I*f all the autonomic systems, breathing is the most abused. We come into the world with this beautiful automatic respiratory machine and our very first action is to push it all of the way to the floor with a mighty cry. From that first cry, we begin to impair its function. There are petulant children who hold their breath, out of spite. At the other end of the spectrum, there is the child who hyperventilates, out of fear or frustration. This is only the beginning!

When we get a little older, we are going to "do it up brown" with tobacco. If that is not enough, we can always go to a nice cozy little bar that has little or no ventilation, and really put the "ole nicotine" to work. Of course, I spent many years cultivating all of these very bad habits. I finally realized what abuse I was perpetrating on my system when

I developed leuko-palakia of the lip, and a cough so extensive I almost burst a blood vessel.

The damage in some respects has been irreparable. I still have a tendency toward shallow breathing, which leads to an insufficiency of oxygen; the other problems have now returned to normal.

If you are wondering why we do not breathe properly, I will list my choice of the four contributory causes to poor respiration.

1. Congenital deformaties
2. Occupational stress and injury
3. Emotional
4. Environmental

The first item is understandable and unavoidable but certainly, in many cases, it is surgically or therapeutically treatable. Many persons are alive today thanks to our improved technology.

Item 2, is where things begin to be people controlled. An analogy of a worker just prior to and during the early industrial revolution may help clarify the issue. Until that time, the majority of the populace were agrarian or farmers who received plenty of exercise, fresh air, and sunshine. With the advent of the Industrial Revolution, more and more people gave up the outdoor life for crowded urban areas. It is interesting to note the probable percentage of urbanites at that time, in the neighborhood of 72 percent, as compared to today's 86 percent in urban society. There is a strong revision of this trend currently occurring throughout the world for the first time in two hundred years, one that will possibly have an eventual impact on our general health during the next two hundred years.

It is easily understood that a physical injury or severe infection will leave scars on the lung tissue that may have a permanent restrictive effect on the autonomic action of the lungs. This restriction might be either in the full pliability of the lung or in its ability to utilize the oxygen in the air sacks. Either of these may be improved with better breathing habits.

The emotional item (3) is one that will affect us all at one time or another, and one over which most of us utilize little or no control. Anxiety, anger, fear, or almost any emotional extreme affects respiration. Here again, the body, in its

beginning is pliable, and as youngsters, we do not suffer physical change as rapidly as we do in our twenties, thirties or forties. This process again increases and deteriorates more rapidly with age and increased pressure.

As for item 4, environmental, surely everyone is aware of air pollution as it exists today. This, too, may be traced back to the Industrial Revolution, for the greater portion of environmental deterioration.

Ironically, man moving to the suburban areas has contributed to air pollution because of his use of the automobile. It is interesting that in the southern California area, where the statistics of auto commuting is almost the highest in the world, the distance traversed daily by commuters has drastically changed over the last thirty years. In 1944, the average worker drove five miles to work; by 1954 the average increased to ten miles; in the '60s it really bounced to almost twenty-five miles. I have not received the figures for the '70s but I would estimate that it is at least thirty-five miles. This is one factor that air pollution experts continue to overlook as statistical information relative to oxidant-level increases. This information is interesting, but unchangeable in our present socio-economic structure. Therefore, if it is irreversible, what can we do to save ourselves? The answer is: learn to breathe!

I wonder how many of us really know how to breathe and exercise our lungs completely. Few people understand and practice this most important body function properly.

The oxygen, inhaled by the lungs, helps in consuming the body's carbohydrates, much as oxygen applied to a fire increases the burning power.

The lungs also supply that ever-so-important oxygen to the cells to sustain life. There can be no ionization process of the blood without oxygen. The ionization process stimulates the flow of neurons (electrical impulses) through the nervous system.

To further explain the physical dynamics of the lungs, some people develop the habit of breathing through the upper lobes of the lung, becoming what I call chest breathers. At the other extreme, we have the person who breathes down through the lower lobes of the lungs, and these people I call stomach breathers. Based upon the construction of the lung, it is wrong to be either a chest or a stomach breather.

The lungs are pliable in order to utilize their flexibility under strain. Take as an example, an auto accident in which a person is behind the steering wheel, pinned tightly with the wheel pushing up under the lower ribs against the diaphragm. In this case, stomach breathing is restricted, but because of the flexibility of the lung, a person may breathe through the upper lobes without much loss of oxygen. The unfortunate part is that we abuse this delicate organ by not expanding it fully when we are in good health.

I mentioned earlier that we are brought into this world with the ability to breathe properly, and the most objective breathing lesson you can receive is to watch an infant. The infant, barring a congenital malformation, breathes down through the diaphragm, then up, into the upper lobes of the chest, thus exercising the entire lung.

The above illustrations in Figure 9-1 are exaggerated. However, the meaning is obvious. At this point I would like to give you a brief physical description of each. Here again, these are general observations that may vary slightly because of other causes and environmental influences.

It is obvious in A of Figure 9-1, that the walls of the abdomen are in constant contraction, thus restricting or constricting the diaphragm or lower part of the lung.

This not only affects the lung, but also the tranverse colon, the lower intestinal tract, the stomach, or the aorta (main artery). This will also cause pressure or tension relative to the pyloric nerves of the abdomen. We thereby find this person prone to emphysema, coronary problems, stomach ulcers, colitis, chronic constipation, hypertension, and many other abdominal oriented problems.

The stomach breather (B) has a relaxed middle region and tends toward obesity. The stomach breather should be wary of upper respiratory problems, varicose veins, upper back and neck, pregnant-woman-back syndrome, and poor

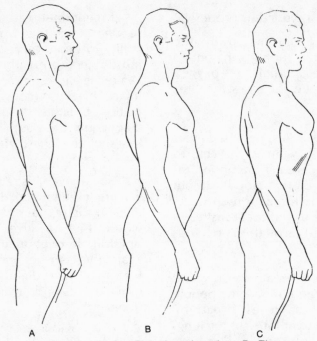

Fig. 9 - 1. A —The chest breather; B—The
stomach breather; C—The normal breather.

circulation in the extremities. These, of course are not all of the related problems, but are the more common ones.

The stomach and chest breather (normal). Will this person suffer no ills at all? Unfortunately, not. While they may enjoy better health, there are of course, many other determining factors involved.

The following is a general psychological image of the three types. The chest breather tends to be hyperactive; aggressive with a bullying attitude; and fretful, with obvious display of emotion. Primarily he is extroverted, but when introverted, he is an extremely insecure individual.

The stomach breather is basical-ly hyperactive, prone to intellectual bullying, and fretful, but internally without indication. Primarily he is introverted, but when extroverted, he may become erratic in his behavior.

The normal breather is an idealist. He does have variations, and as I mentioned before, environmental and inherent characteristics do produce changes. Throughout the centuries, writers and artists have depicted the miserly as thin, drawn wretches, and the jovial as rotund cherubs, which has had a certain amount of fact, but extremes were used to illustrate the point.

In my work I have developed a sensitivity to muscle tone. I believe this tells the story more factually than the visual appearance. It is not uncommon for a person coming to me for the first time to discover that they are not breathing deeply enough. I detect this by the pliability of the tissue. The transformation that occurs when a person begins breathing properly (deeply) is amazing. With the increased oxygen supply, the tissue comes alive and expands, rather than contracts and is spasmodic. I have no laboratory proof, but from years of observation, when tension occurs across the shoulders, this restricts respiration by affecting the thoracic vertebrae (refer to Chart I, page 00), and thereby irritating the sympathetic or parasympathetic nerves, activating or retarding respiration.

We have now studied the three basic types of breathers. Now, certain changes may be brought about through corrective breathing. I will use only the chest breather and the stomach breather, as they are extreme cases.

The chest breather is inclined to hypertension and coronaries. As previously discussed, this is because of muscular contraction of the abdominal wall muscles.

To relieve this condition, lie down on either the floor or a very firm mattress and follow these steps:

1. Place your right hand on the abdomen with the palm over the navel.
2. Push the abdomen up, so that the hand is thrust upward. This is done with the muscle of the abdomen—not the hand.
3. After the muscles are pushing the abdomen upward, inhale slowly, taking the air down to the stomach. When done properly, you will feel a ballooning under the right hand.
4. This should be repeated ten times, and each time you should try and force the air down lower than the position of the right hand. Eventually, you should breath into the area just above the bladder (urinary).
5. This exercise should be done first thing in the morning, once during the midday, late afternoon, early evening, and again just before sleep.
   Repeat: Each time, take ten breathes.

There is a two-fold process occurring with this exercise: (1) relaxation and (2) blood ionization.

Look again at Figure 9-1 (B). As you remember, the stomach breather does most of his breathing through the abdomen and has respiratory and circulatory problem tendencies.

Finding myself in this category some years ago, I will relate my own experience.

For the greater portion of my life I was a stomach breather. When my experiment began, my pulse was 55; blood pressure 118/68; thirty-four years old, and weighed two-hundred fifty pounds. The experiment lasted three years, but the transformation occurred within one and one-half years. It took that long to condition my natural stomach-breathing tendency. During this entire period, my diet remained the same. We had two children at the start of the experiment, and the third was born after the first three months of my starting it. There were no money problems or any undue pressures during the three years. A financial crisis had occurred about six years previously. However, I suffered no physical change from that. I would have to say, this was the most carefree time of my life.

It was quite difficult for me to change from stomach breathing to chest breathing. The ribcage was virtually inflexible, and I therefore kept reverting back to the stomach breathing. After approximately four months, it became more natural. I also noted, I had a great deal more energy. Another fringe benefit was that of streamlining. At the beginning, I was pear-shaped, but as time progressed, the round shoulders started squaring-off; the stomach pulled-in; and even though I had added weight (approximately ten pounds when I stopped smoking), my waist was actually an inch narrower.

After the first six months, I really began to notice changes. I found myself not being able to sit still. I, who had been sedentary all my life, was finding out how the other half lived. I found that I was more argumentative, a feeling quite unusual to me. These were only the beginning of the changes.

In my high school days, I had had a great passion for football, so much so, that my coach was sure I could win an athletic scholarship.

This was based on my size and the assumption that I had the aggressiveness needed. I had the size, but not the aggressiveness. If I then had had the benefit of my knowledge now, I would have, no doubt, pursued pro-football. A couple of years after changing to chest breathing, I had an opportunity to play sandlot football and found out that at thirty-six, I had more power and drive than I had had at seventeen. In those younger days, I wanted to punt and be a place-kicker, but could not get the distance or accuracy. At thirty-six, I found I could punt fifty yards with good control. The greatest change though, was the confidence that I could do the things I wanted to do and they were easy. At this time, my pulse had risen to 65; the blood pressure 140/80.

As time progressed, everything was intensified with my pulse reaching 72 and the blood pressure 155/85 at the end of three years.

The thing I did not count on was spending the next eleven years getting the pulse and pressure down. Actually, it was only an additional three years to seriously work at lowering both. At the age of forty-nine years, my pulse is 65 and blood pressure 132/78. I no doubt could make it lower, but then I would loose the drive once more. Oh yes, my weight is now 265 pounds.

The moral of this chapter is that it does not take a genius to learn the proper way to breathe; just common sense, practice, and concentration.

QUESTIONS
CHAPTER IX

1. Name as many ways as you can that we damage our respiratory system.
   Ans. Page 117.

2. What are the four contributory causes to poor respiration?
   Ans. Page 117.

3. In what way did world industralization indirectly effect respiration?
   Ans. Page 118.

4. The third contributory cause to poor respiration, the emotional factor, can be summed up with one psychological term. Name it.
   Ans. Page 118.

5. What was the average mileage of the communter - worker in Southern California in 1944?
   Ans. Page 118.

6. Describe in what way the respiration process influences the nervous system.
   Ans. Page 119.

7. Name the three types of 'breathers'.
   Ans. Page 119.

8. What are the many detrimental effects caused by the "Chest Breather"?
   Ans. Page 119.

9. Describe the "Stomach Breather".
   Ans. Page 119.

10. Name two emotional traits of the "Chest Breather".
    Ans. Page 120.

11. Can a physical transformation occur when improper breathing is corrected?
    Ans. Page 120.

12. What does proper muscle-tone indicate?
    Ans. Page 120.

13. Review Illustration   - Page 82 (Spinal Vertebrae) and name the vertebrae effected by the lung.

   Ans. Pages 82.

14. How many exercises or steps are indicated to relieve the conditions created by the "Chest Breather"?

   Ans. Page 121.

15. What is the two-fold process occuring with the exercise in question 14?

   Ans. Page 121

16. From my personal example stated within this chapter, is it possible to change and control pulse and blood-pressure?

   Ans. Page 121.

17. Review my age, pulse, blood-pressure and weight at the beginning of my experiment and compare two years later.

   Ans. Page 121.

18. Does your blood-pressure effect your "drive"?

   Ans. Page 122.

CHAPTER TEN
CONCLUSION

This book has not been written to shake all of your previously conceived ideas about pain and its relief. This book has been written with the intention of broadening your scope to analyze possible causes of your pain, and the relief you may give yourself.

I have purposely avoided the pure concept of Shiatsu because of its very deep philosophical nature and unusual utilization of the periphial nerve reflexes. You have been given in this book a starting point to determine whether you choose to go beyond this beginning.

We have heard many claims about the benefits of Shiatsu and Acupuncture but you must remember, these, as in all other therapies, medications, and surgeries are not always 100 percent. We are, many times, left in doubt as to the total efficiency of any of the healing arts or sciences.

It is my interpretation of the ancients, i.e., the Egyptians, Greeks, and Chinese, that they said that no one branch of healing is complete and that the body must be treated as a single unit. Unfortunately, this is not the attitude today.

The future of medicine is closely aligned with the healing arts of the past and the two are only now beginning to converge. How complete and when this marriage will be remains to be seen, but I do foresee in the not-too-distant future people like myself, properly trained, being acknowledged in this country and utilized as special technicians in a clinical type situation, and available to the recognized medical world.

Shiatsu is the oldest form of physical therapy in recorded form in existence today.

This recorded history is noted nearly three thousand years ago in

Central China. It was then called *Tien-An*. This was during the Yellow Emperor's Dynasty, about 500 B.C. The early recording coincides with the first mention of Acupuncture, which came from northern China. Both became an integral part of Chinese medicine, no doubt because of their parallel theories of peripheral neurology.

During the sixth century A.D., *Tien-An* was introduced to the Japanese and was called Shiatsu. Both Shiatsu and Acupuncture are practiced in Japan, but of the two, Shiatsu is more popular because of its flexibility and adaptation to more specific and minute aches and pains, as herein outlined.

The total picture of Shiatsu cannot be presented or understood in book form any more than the intricacies of medicine can totally be learned without proper academic training.

During the Edo Period (1830) in Japanese history, western medicine or allopathic medical practice was introduced. Since that time, many medical schools comparable to American and European schools have been developed. This Euro-American influence dominated Japanese medical thinking until the middle twentieth century, at which time a revival of Shiatsu was started by Dr. Tokujiro Namikosh, founder of the Nippon Shiatsu Institute.

It was Dr. Namikoshi who was responsible for national legislation in Japan to reinstate Shiatsu as an accepted science, with the national licensing board.

A point of interest is the stationing of Shiatsu practitioners in the Capitol building while the legislators are in session, as a deterent to coronaries and strokes during legislative sessions.

The Japanese medical profession accepts Shiatsu in somewhat the same way osteopaths and physical therapists are acknowledged in the United States. The Nippon Shiatsu Institute has graduated over 20,000 students, of which I was one of the first foreigners to receive my papers. I also had the pleasure of working on the first English translation of Dr. Namikoshi's book on Shiatsu.

We had three prominent American celebrities taking treatments from Dr. Namikoshi when I attended the institute in the '50s. They were: Marilyn Monroe, Joe DiMaggio, and Lefty O'Doul. There were many more, but these were the important names at that time.

For centuries Shiatsu, like many other sciences was a religious art form. It was introduced by the Buddhist monks and remained under their direction until the 1930s when Dr. Namikoshi began researching the ancient Chinese texts and evolving a crude scientific theory. The results of Shiatsu were evident, but existing scientific theories were unsupportive.

There is, at the present time, considerable work being done in the field of neurology in the Orient. Dr. Kim Bong, of Korea, has discovered a bioelectric corpuscle in the blood stream, which is thought to be the connecting link in the Oriental meridians. Energy flows, meridians, *Ki* points, or *tsubo* have been referred to in earlier sections of this book. I will now give you my theory on their function.

Let us first analyze the few existing facts that we do have on Shiatsu.

1. Tension is relieved.
2. Circulation is improved.
3. Lactic acid (neural waste) is changed to glycogen (energy cells).

These three points are irrefutable. But how important are they? Very, if you relate these points to modern allopathic medicine and their use of tranquilizers, muscle relaxants, and vasodialators to achieve these goals. In regard to item 3, I would say the amphetamine (uppers) drugs produce somewhat the same effect with hallucinations as an added extra.

I would like to reiterate the fact that Oriental medicine and therapy treat the body as a *single unified unit* i.e., glandular, vascular, neural, muscle and bone structure, the internal organs, and the emotions. The impact that emotions and physical stress have on our bodies is strong, and this, in turn, leads us to the Yin and Yang theory of Oriental medicine.

The Yin and Yang might be referred to the Hyde and Jekyll; female and male; weak and strong; or bad and good syndromes, and is used as a subjective personality characteristic in psychology. I am not interested psychologically, other than the physical manifestations produced by tensions of these types and their referred effects on the autonomic nervous system.

Oriental medicine applies the same theory to the organs of the body with a further subdivision, or relationship of man to his environment, by analyzing the various systems of the body as these systems relate to the five fundamental elements of man, i.e., wood, fire, earth, metal, and water.

Chart II shows these five environmental fundamentals, plus the five fundamental systems of the body.

The nervous system (C) including the emotions; it is the prime system because of its influence on the other four systems. In other words, removing the nervous system will cause the other four systems to fail.

It is necessary to modify the original macrocosm concept slightly in order to place an emphasis on the portion I consider to be the dominant factor, since the others are relevant to it.

I consider earth (A) primary to the other elements, as it either contributes to or receives from the other four.

The ancient Chinese macrocosms differed slightly from mine in that all elements and systems were equal and related by assimilation, i.e., wood, fire, earth, metal, and water, or blue, red, yellow, white, and black.

I have placed the body macrocosm in the macrocosm as the five systems* (endocrine system is not included) as shown in Chart II. The main objective is to illustrate man's relationship to his environment and the biological reactions thereby produced.

Chart II

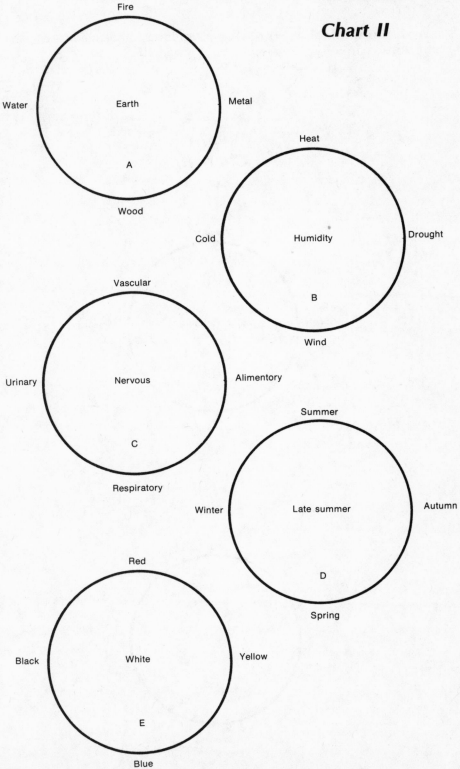

Along with this, the five emotions: anxiety, anger, joy, sadness, and fear, are placed on Chart III.

Chart III

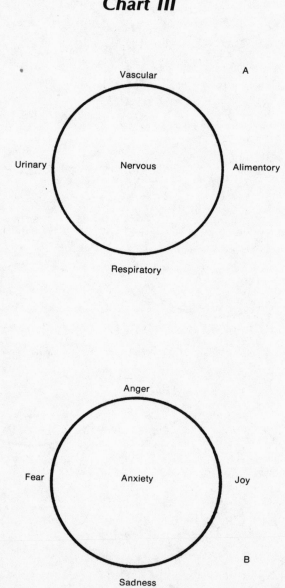

In Chart IV, the nervous system (A) is dissected into five functional divisions; and the neuron (B) is divided into a functional system.

Chart IV

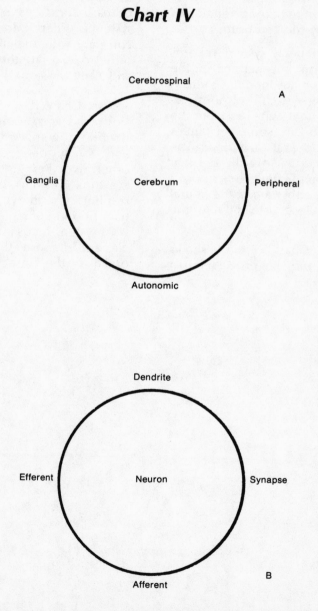

Why did I select the above sections for each systematic breakdown? Let's start with the cerebrum. The cerebrum is the generator, or dynamo for the other four systems. It is also affected by them, i.e., the cerebrospinal system is the body switchboard, its functioning subject to final correlation of all systems by the cerebrum.

The peripheral system records and carries out the actions of the cerebrum. The autonomic system is the stabilizing system, but does respond to constant agitation from the cerebrum, or in some instances chronic peripheral irritation. The ganglion are trunk distributors that have a direct effect on neuron transmission, either along the neural trunk or a close proximity to the autonomic system.

Part B in (Chart IV) simple shows the neuron and the processes that motivate it. I will not delve any deeper at this time, other than to say that this is the submicrocosm of the nervous system. This may be a bit confusing to those who have not studied neurology and Oriental medicine, but it is sufficient to understand that we are breaking the primary functions of the different systemic orders into five parts that correlate with the five elements in order to associate them with the Yin and Yang division.

In Chart II, C shows the five body systems, omitting the endocrine system, which is ductless and totally dependent upon the other five. Remembering the five systems (vascular, alimentary, respiratory, urinary), with the dominant position being held by the nervous system, let us make another circle and impose the microcosmic organs of the Yin or passive organs.

Chart V

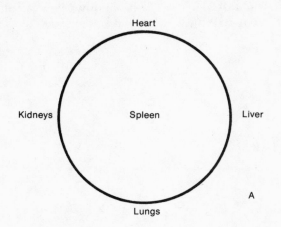

Heart

Kidneys   Spleen   Liver

Lungs

A

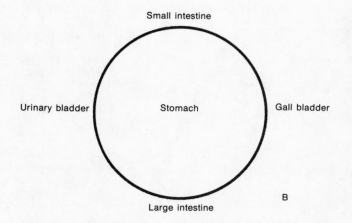

Small intestine

Urinary bladder   Stomach   Gall bladder

Large intestine

B

The other circle shows the active organs of the Yang.

I am showing you these old Chinese microcosomic breakdowns to give you a basic foundation. This is oversimplified to a great extent, as this is an extremely complex study – in total.

At this point, I will now introduce a new field of my own by combining basic Chinese medica macrocosom and microcosom, a breakdown of emotions, and the nervous system.

Chart VI

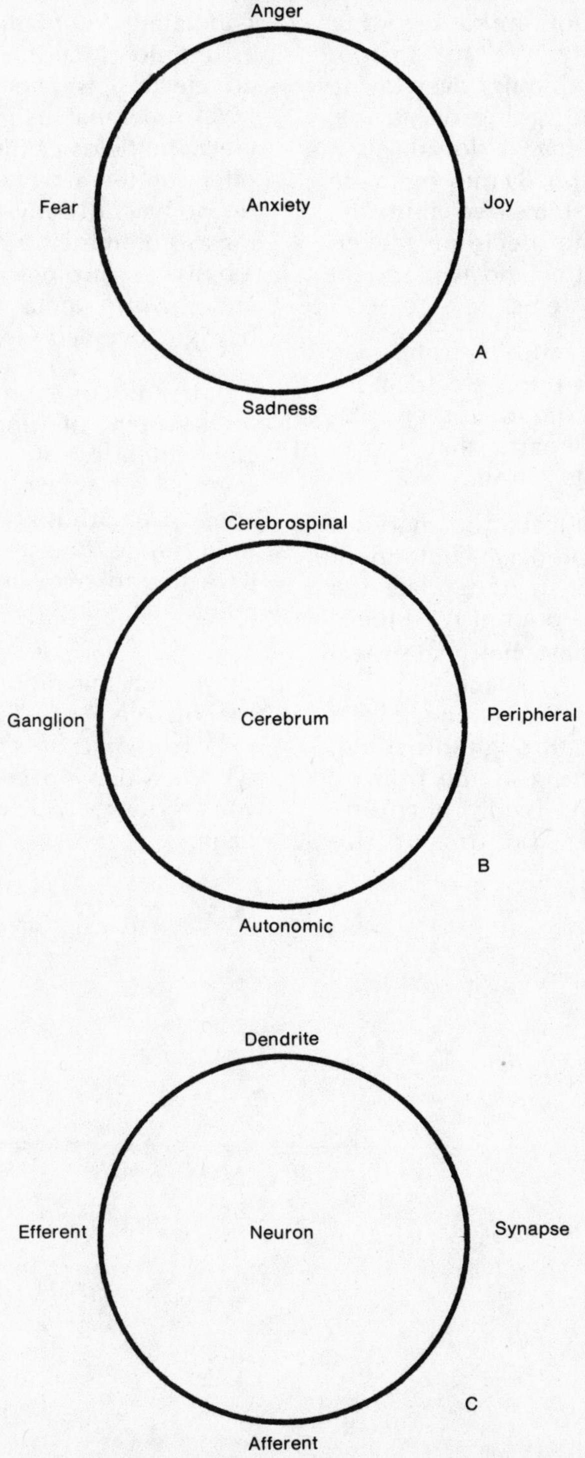
Anger
Fear
Anxiety
Joy
A
Sadness
Cerebrospinal
Ganglion
Cerebrum
Peripheral
B
Autonomic
Dendrite
Efferent
Neuron
Synapse
C
Afferent

The one emotion that is with us always is anxiety. We are anxious over losing or winning, over loving and being loved, going or staying, etc. No matter what we do, anxiety is the prime emotion. By moving to the transmission systems we find the cerebrum is the decision maker, prime coordinator, and respondent for the other systems.

Progressing another step, we reach the neuron, the electrical innervator, relay component, and the four functional parts that move, divert, or stop its action.

Having reduced the nervous system to its primary component (the neuron), let us now relate the neurons to conception. Isn't it feasible to assume that when male spermazoa come in contact with the female egg, the first connection is bioelectric; then through this union, the neurons, acting as the primary nervous system, begin decoding DNA and RNA factors of the copulating cells? Following the same assumption (that the first signs of life are electric), is it not also reasonable to assume that magnetic or strong electrical fields of force will have an effect on the activity of the neuron decoding the body factors? Assuming this premise is true, we now have a basis for astrological, atmospheric and environmental effects on the newly conceived life.

This discourse has finally led us to the point of supporting the ancient theories of astrological and seasonal effects on the human nervous system, thus giving credence to the Chinese theories of medicine, as it relates to man and his environment.

It is at this point appropriate to introduce the Yin and Yang relationship of the endocrine system, which is passive, and the nervous system, which is the active Yang.

Yin

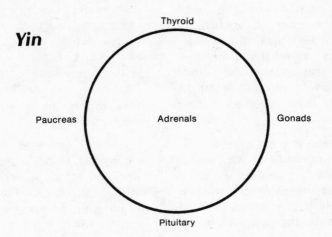

Yang

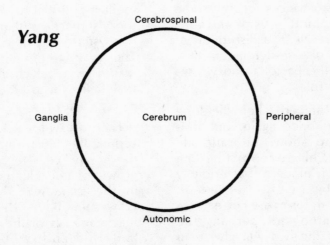

Chart VII

In the endocrine system, the adrenals are the key glands because of the stimulus they give the remainder of the system. Here again between the Yin and Yang, we may develop a conflict of the two systems. As an example, a chronic irritation may develop in the vesical nerve plexus, either from muscle strain or neural inflammation and become chronic. This may in turn, lead to a disfunction of the bladder or sex organs.

The same example applies for all of the plexus of the body with none receiving reater abuse than the gastric plexus of the stomach; this in turn, not only has an effect on the stomach, but also the pancreas, liver, and spleen.

To the end that the nervous system has come into conflict with the endocrine system (Yin) and another Yang system (the stomach), and the second Yin system of the spleen. Disturbances of this type affect the metabolism and undoubtedly result in a disruption of the body's disease-fighting factors, permitting the bacteria and viruses to gain control.

I have indeed taken the long way around once again, but it is necessary to show the rationale behind the Chinese form of healing and that of modern bacteriology developed by scientists like Pasteur. Certainly both forms are correct to a limited degree and perhaps the marriage of the two will give us a more complete understanding. Virtually everyone has experienced physical changes as the weather modulates from one season to the other. The atmospheric change affect the sensory nerves as well as the autonomic system, and be relating macrocosom theory an making man's body a part of his environment and then by placing th body functions into the Yin (inactive and Yang (active) organs an systems, we have an antagonisti situation with a firm basis fo deviations in the defensive antibod mechanism.

My objective in this portion o the book is to correlate related por tions of both approaches to healing and possibly to stimulate another' thinking to carry on the process to logical conclusion.

Bigoted thinking has persisted for centuries and has prevented successful union of therapies. I hope it is on its way out. Within the nex twenty-five years, I think we will see a drastic change in the practice o medicine. It will no more resemble today's practices than our present day systems resemble witch doctors The vistas are exciting in nucleu medicine, bioelectric therapy, and new fields yet to be developed.

Recently I saw a report by Dr Becker of Syracuse University concerning the electrical stimulation of nerves and cells to regenerate the growth of a new limb on a rat, much in the same way the chameleon grows new limbs. Dr. Becker feels that mammals of the higher orders had this ability, but with the development of other portions of the brain, sacrificed the ability of cell regeneration.

It is curious how many of the myths of yesteryear are now being substantiated by scientific research today in a clear and logical way. Is this possibly the return of an earlier portion of a superior knowledge developed in antiquity?

Biologists are saying today that we should live seven-score and ten years in relatively good health, which is somewhat more than our present life span. I believe that man in lost generations evolved to a high intellectual plane, and we are now beginning to regain those heights.

We are still amazed at the engineering capabilities of the Egyptians and Mayan civilizations. These, of course, are the obvious physical examples for us to see. What of the strides attained by the Hebrew, Greek, Hindu, Roman, and Chinese cultures, particularly in the spiritual and philosophical arenas. There are indeed many unanswered questions involving the history of cultures past and present to be resolved. They can broaden our present understanding and knowledge to project for ourselves a more complete awareness for living.

CHAPTER X

1. What was my reason for writing this book?
   Ans. Page 125

2. The "pure concept of "SHIATSU" was avoided for a specific purpose. What was that purpose?
   Ans. Page 125.

3. "No one branch of healing is complete and the body must be treated as a single unit.", is an interpretation of the ancients message, is this the attitude today?
   Ans. Page 125.

4. What was the Chinese term for Shiatsu?
   Ans. Page 125.

5. In what century was "Tien An" introduced in Japan?
   Ans. Page 126.

6. What is aleopathic medical practice and when was it introduced in Japan?
   Ans. Page 126.

7. In what way does the Japanese medical profession accept Shiatsu?
   Ans. Page 126.

8. Name three irrefutable effects of physical change as a result of proper use of Shiatsu.
   Ans. Page 127.

9. Are the results, as indicated in question 8, comparable to those produced with modern aleopathic medicine and their use of drugs? Which drugs?
   Ans. Page 127.

10. What are the "simple" descriptions of the Yin and Yang syndromes?
    Ans. Page 127.

11. Review and understand the relationship between seasons and certain types of rather chronic disorders as indicated in Chart II - page 127.
    Ans. Page 127.

12. What reason did I give for varying the ancient Chinese Macrocosm of the five elements?
    Ans. Page 128.

13. What are the functions of the five divisions of the nervous system?
    Ans. Page 128.

14. Name the prime emotion that is with us always.

    Ans. Page 131

15. Explain the conception hypothesis expressed in this chapter.

    Ans. Page 131.

16. In what way does the conception hypothesis relate to the ancient Chinese theories of medicine?

    Ans. Page 132.

17. Which organs might be involved with an irritation of the vesical nerve plexus?

    Ans. Page 132.

18. The conflict between the nervous system and the Yin and Yang organs creates what problem for the body?

    Ans. Page 132.

19. Describe Dr. Becker's theory regarding regeneration.

    Ans. Page 133.